GCSE Edexcel 360Science
Physics
The Workbook

This book is for anyone doing **GCSE Edexcel 360Science Physics**.

It's full of **tricky questions**... each one designed to make you **sweat** — because that's the only way you'll get any **better**.

There are questions to see **what facts** you know. There are questions to see how well you can **apply those facts**. And there are questions to see what you know about **how science works**.

It's also got some daft bits in to try and make the whole experience at least vaguely entertaining for you.

What CGP is all about

Our sole aim here at CGP is to produce the highest quality books — carefully written, immaculately presented and dangerously close to being funny.

Then we work our socks off to get them out to you — at the cheapest possible prices.

Contents

Published by Coordination Group Publications Ltd.

Editors:
Amy Boutal, Katherine Craig, Gemma Hallam, Sarah Hilton, Kate Houghton,
Laurence Stamford, Julie Wakeling, Sarah Williams.

Contributors:
Tony Alldridge, Steve Coggins, Mark A Edwards, Andrew Furze, Dr Giles R Greenway,
Jason Howell, Frederick Langridge, Barbara Mascetti, John Myers, Andy Rankin,
Pat Szczesniak, Paul Warren, Jim Wilson.

ISBN: 978 1 84146 468 8

With thanks to Ian Francis and Glenn Rogers for the proofreading.

Groovy website: www.cgpbooks.co.uk

Printed by Elanders Hindson Ltd, Newcastle upon Tyne.
Jolly bits of clipart from CorelDRAW®

Electric Current

Q1 Use the words in the box to fill in the gaps. Use each word **once only**.

> more
> voltage
> resistance
> less
> current
> force

a) The flow of electrons around a circuit is called the ....

b) .... is the '............................' that pushes the current around the circuit.

c) If you increase the voltage, ... current will flow.

d) If you increase the ...., ... current will flow.

Q2 Here are three different circuits, **A – C**. All the **cells** and **resistors** are **identical**.

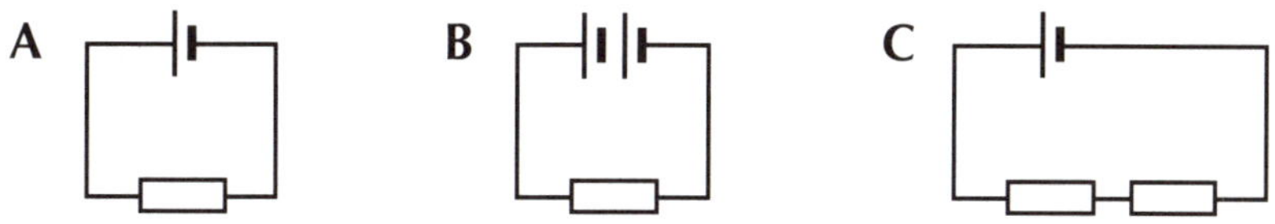

A B C

Write down the letters representing the circuits in order of **increasing current**. ..../ ..../ ....

Q3 The diagram shows three traces on the same **cathode ray oscilloscope** (CRO). The settings are the **same** in each case.

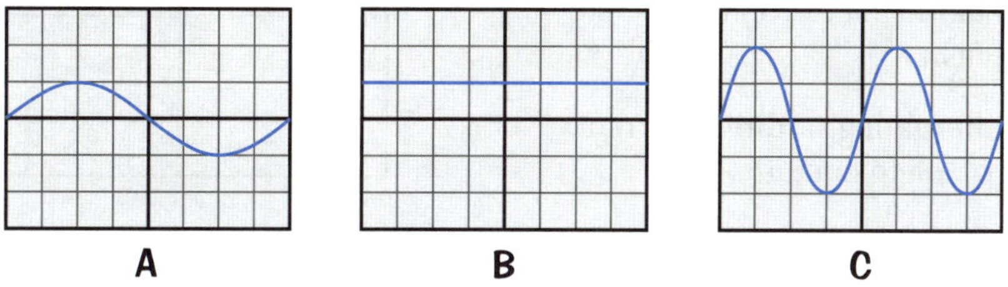

A **B** **C**

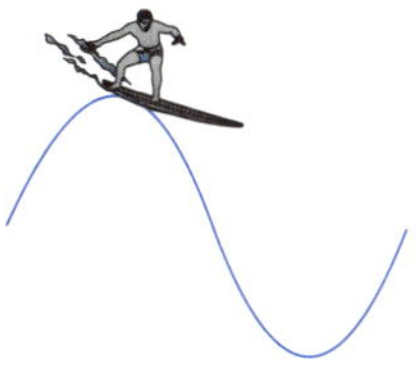

Write down the **letter** of the trace that shows:

a) the highest frequency AC ..../ **b)** direct current ..../ **c)** the lowest AC voltage ....

Q4 Scientists **decided** which way current flows around an electrical circuit before electrons were discovered.

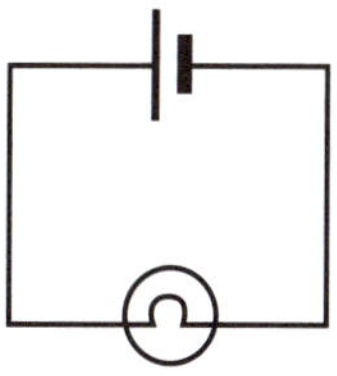

a) Draw arrows on the diagram on the right to show the direction of **conventional current**.

b) **Which way** would the **electrons** be moving?

....

Q5 Trisha has connected a CRO to a **battery** to measure its voltage.

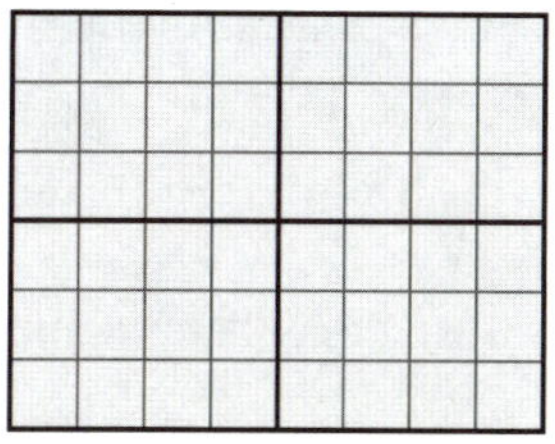

a) On this diagram of a CRO screen, **draw** what Trisha might see.

b) **Name another power source** that would produce this shape.

....

Generating Electricity

Q1 Use the words in the box to **fill in the blanks** in these two paragraphs about generating electricity.

| moving | electromagnetic | magnet | coil | induction |
| alternating | voltage | reverses | magnetic | complete |

You can create a .... across an electrical conductor by .... a

magnet near the conductor. This is called ....

In simple generators, this is usually achieved by rotating a .... near a

.... of wire. The generator produces an .... current when it is

connected up to a .... circuit. The current alternates since the direction of the

.... field .... every time the magnet rotates by half a turn.

Q2 The diagram on the right shows the trace produced when a **coil** is connected to a cathode ray oscilloscope and a **magnet** is **rotated nearby**.

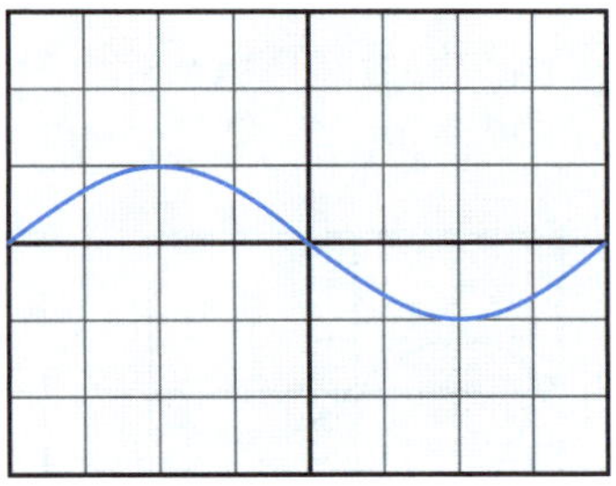

a) On the diagram, draw what the trace would look like if the magnet was rotated **faster**.

b) Would the coil produce **alternating** or **direct** current if it was connected to a complete circuit? **Explain** your answer.

....

....

c) Apart from rotating the magnet faster, what **three other things** could you do to make the maximum voltage **larger**?

1. ....

2. ....

3. ....

Q3 The lights on Sebastian's bicycle are powered by a **dynamo**. Explain why the bicycle lights dim as he slows down.

....

....

Generating Electricity

Q4 Decide whether the following AC generators would produce a **higher**, a **lower** or **the same** voltage as the generator in the box. Circle the correct answer.

a) More coils

higher / lower / the same

b) Stronger magnet

higher / lower / the same

c) Slower rotation

higher / lower / the same

Q5 Moving a **magnet** inside a **coil of wire** produces a trace on a cathode ray oscilloscope.

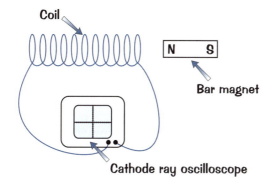

Coil

N S

Bar magnet

Cathode ray oscilloscope

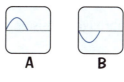

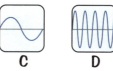

Traces on oscilloscope

A   B

C   D

When the magnet was pushed inside the coil, trace A was produced on the screen.

a) Explain how trace B could be produced.

....

b) Explain how trace C could be produced.

....

c) Explain how trace D could be produced.

....

d) Explain how energy is transferred from the moving magnet to the oscilloscope.

....

....

Top Tips: You can tell why people thought electricity was magic in the olden days — wave a magnet near some wire and hey presto... you get some electricity. Make sure you know what to change to make the voltage generated change and you'll generate lots of marks.

Current, Voltage and Resistance

Q1   Match up these items from a standard test circuit with the **correct description** and **symbol**.

ITEM	DESCRIPTION	SYMBOL
Cell	The item you're testing.	—(A)—
Variable Resistor	Provides the voltage.	(resistor with arrow)
Component	Used to alter the current.	—||—
Voltmeter	Measures the current.	—(V)—
Ammeter	Measures the voltage.	—[ ]—

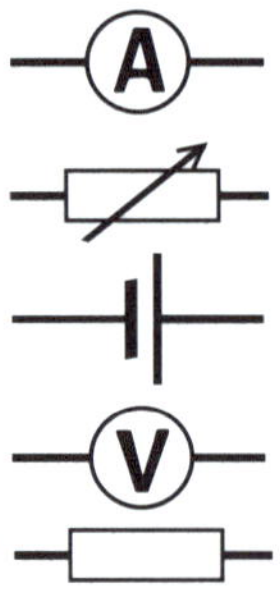

Q2   Indicate whether these statements are **true** or **false**.
Write out a **correct version** of the false statements.

		True	False
a)	An ammeter should always be connected in parallel with a component.	☐	☐
b)	A voltmeter should always be connected in series with a component.	☐	☐
c)	The resistance of a filament lamp decreases as it gets hot.	☐	☐
d)	The current through a resistor at constant temperature is proportional to the voltage.	☐	☐

....

....

....

Q3   The graph below shows **V-I curves** for four resistors.

$$\text{Gradient} = \frac{\text{vertical change}}{\text{horizontal change}}$$

a)   Write down the equation that relates voltage, current and resistance.

....

b)   The resistance of each component is equal to 1/gradient of its V-I curve.

    i)   Which resistor has the highest resistance?   ....

    ii)   Calculate the gradient of the line for resistor B.

....

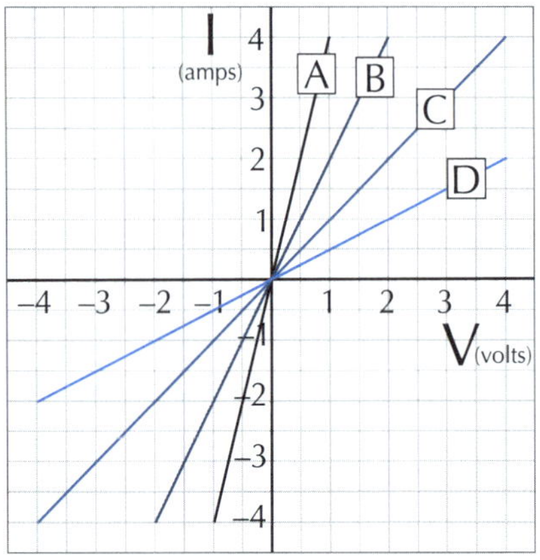

    iii)   Calculate the resistance of resistor B.

....

Current, Voltage and Resistance

Q4 Fill in the **missing values** in the table.

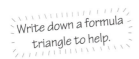

Write down a formula triangle to help.

Voltage (V)	Current (A)	Resistance (Ω)
6	2	
8		2
	3	3
4	8	
2		4
	0.5	2

Q5 Peter tested **three components** using a standard test circuit. The table below shows his results.

Voltage (V)	−4.0	−3.0	−2.0	−1.0	0.0	1.0	2.0	3.0	4.0
Component **A** current (A)	−2.0	−1.5	−1.0	−0.5	0.0	0.5	1.0	1.5	2.0
Component **B** current (A)	0.0	0.0	0.0	0.0	0.0	0.2	1.0	2.0	4.5
Component **C** current (A)	−4.0	−3.5	−3.0	−2.0	0.0	2.0	3.0	3.5	4.0

a) Draw a **V-I graph** for each component on the axes below.

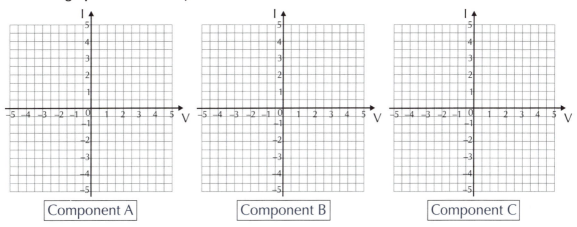

Component A   Component B   Component C

b) Complete Peter's **conclusions**:

Component **A** is a ....

Component **B** is a ....

Component **C** is a ....

Q6 Helen set up the circuit below:

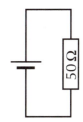

a) Draw a second resistor in **parallel** with the first.

b) If the resistor you have just drawn has a resistance of 5 Ω, explain what will happen to the total resistance of the circuit.

....

....

Varying Resistance and Sensors

Q1   Tick the boxes to show whether the following statements are **true** or **false**.

		True	False
a)	LDRs and thermistors are types of **variable** resistor.	☐	☐
b)	An LDR has a **high** resistance in very **bright** light.	☐	☐
c)	The resistance of a thermistor **increases** as the temperature **decreases**.	☐	☐
d)	An LDR could be part of a useful thermostat.	☐	☐

Q2   After each of the following sentences, write "**LDR**" if it's about an LDR, "**thermistor**" if it's about a thermistor, or "**both**" if it's about both.

a)   Could be used as part of a thermostat. ....

b)   Could be used as a light sensor. ....

c)   Changes its resistance in response to conditions around it. ....

d)   Would have a high resistance in a warm dark room. ....

e)   Would have a low resistance in a warm dark room. ....

Q3   A **temperature sensor** was connected to a **data logger** and used to investigate the inside of a **fridge**. The results are shown on the right.

a)   What do you think happened after **2 hours** and after **4 hours**?

....

b)   Suggest why you **couldn't** carry out this experiment using a normal hand-held thermometer.

....

....

Q4   Ron is on holiday taking photos with his brand new digital camera. Whether it's night or day, he's amazed to find his camera knows **how long** the shutter should stay open to let the right amount of light in.

a)   What type of variable resistor is used in camera shutter circuits? ....

b)   Explain how the sensor controls the time the shutter stays open for.

....

....

....

<u>*Varying Resistance and Sensors*</u>

Q5   Helen set up an experiment to see how the **resistance** of an **LDR** varies with **light intensity**.

Here are her results:

light intensity / W/m²	5	10	20	30	40	50
resistance / Ω	6000	3500	2000	1500	1200	1000

a) Helen's teacher said that she should have **repeated** her readings. **Explain** why this is useful.

....

....

b) **Plot a graph** of Helen's results on the grid below.

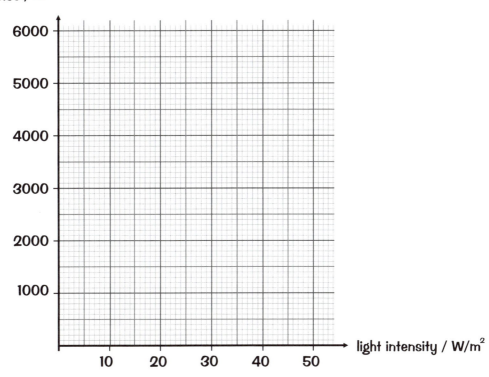

A timing circuit using an LDR can be used to send an electrical signal after a fixed time.
Helen investigated a timing circuit using her LDR.
She found that the time interval (in seconds) = 0.00001 × R where R is the resistance of her LDR in ohms.

c) **i)** Find the time interval when the light intensity is 50 W/m².

....

ii) Find the time interval when the light intensity is 25 W/m².

....

8

Batteries and Their Uses

Q1   Complete the following passage on **dry-cell batteries**, choosing from the words below.

cheaper	rechargeable	dry	dispose	longer
waste	recycling	expensive	reuse	

Dry-cell batteries are .... and last .... than a single charge

of a rechargeable battery, but once they have been used once you have to

.... of them. This can be a .... of resources but there are

ways of .... them.

Q2   Many modern devices like mobile phones use **rechargeable** batteries.

a)   Write down **two** advantages of using rechargeable instead of dry-cell batteries.

1. ....

2. ....

b)   What is the 'memory effect'?

....

....

c)   Some rechargeable batteries contain a highly toxic chemical called cadmium.
How must these batteries be disposed of?

....

Q3 a)   Fill in the boxes to complete the definition of **battery capacity**.

Capacity (in ⬚⬚⬚⬚⬚⬚⬚⬚) = ⬚⬚⬚⬚⬚⬚⬚⬚ (in A) × ⬚⬚⬚⬚⬚⬚ (in ⬚⬚⬚⬚⬚⬚)

b)   A car battery can supply a current of 5 A for 15 hours. What is its capacity?

....

c)   A 1.5 A h calculator battery can power the calculator for 30 hours.
What current does the calculator use?

....

d)   A remote-controlled car uses an electric current of 2 A.
For how long can a 6 A h battery power the car?

....

<u>*Batteries and Their Uses*</u>

Q4 Dura-batt pride themselves on producing long-life batteries. The graph shows the results when their best battery provides a current of **1.5 A** until it goes flat.

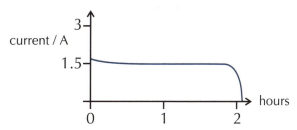

a) Approximate the **capacity** of this battery.

....

b) On the diagram **draw the graph** you would expect to get if the battery provided a **current** of **3 A**.

Q5 Simon is a robot geek and is going to compete on 'Robot Legends'. He needs to find out how much it will cost to power his robot, which needs a total battery capacity of **30 A h.**

a) i) If a dry-cell has a capacity of **1.5 A h** then how many dry-cell batteries will the robot need?

....

....

ii) If each dry-cell battery costs **£1.50** then what will be the total cost of powering the robot?

....

The capacity of a rechargeable battery is **3 A h.**

b) i) How many times will the battery have to be recharged?

....

ii) The cost of electricity is **10p** for each recharge.
How much will it cost for all of the recharging?

....

iii) The uncharged battery costs **£4.00** to buy.
How much would it cost to power the robot using this battery?

....

c) Because Simon is pretty broke, he wants to power his robot as **cheaply** as possible.
Which type of battery should he use?

....

<u>*Top Tips:*</u> Rechargeable batteries — not always as good for the environment as they might sound. Make sure you know the pros and cons of each type of battery and how to work out battery capacity.

New Technology and the Modern World

Q1 Use the words in the box to **complete the blanks** in the following passage.

| melting | zero | superconductors | low | high |
| hot | wasting | electrical | magnets | |

Some materials have .... electrical resistance when they are at really

.... temperatures. We call these materials ....

Unlike normal wires, they can carry really .... currents without getting

.... (so .... energy as heat) or even ....

Superconductors were just a scientific curiosity for many years until they were used to

produce very powerful .... which are used, e.g., in particle accelerators.

Q2 Electricity has transformed everyday life. Complete the table to show how each task was done **before** electricity was discovered, and how it's done with electricity. The first one has been done for you.

Task	With electricity	Without electricity
Illumination	light bulb	candle / lantern
Cooking		
Keeping food fresh		
Home entertainment		
Washing clothes		
Communication		

Q3 Materials can only superconduct if they're cooled to extremely **low temperatures**.

a) Why is this a disadvantage?

....

....

b) What advantage would there be in making the **electricity power lines** of the National Grid out of **superconductors**?

....

....

New Technology and the Modern World

Q4 Maglev trains are the fastest trains in the world.

a) Explain how the discovery of superconductors has led to the creation of the Maglev train.

....

....

b) Why can Maglev trains travel so much faster than ordinary trains?

....

Q5 Here are two graphs showing data about **computer microprocessors** since 1990:

a) Which of the following statements can you **deduce** from these graphs? Circle the correct letter(s) A-D.

I.e. which statements do the graphs tell you directly and for definite?

A The more transistors a processor has, the greater its speed.

B Both the number of transistors per chip and the processor speed have increased since 1990.

C Electric components are getting smaller.

D Computers are getting cheaper.

b) Explain how the graphs could **suggest** that electric components are **getting smaller**.

....

....

c) Which statement about the speed of the processors is **correct**? **Circle the correct letter, A – C.**

A the speed is increasing at an increasing rate

B the speed is increasing at a decreasing rate

C the speed is increasing linearly

d) Explain why the **shape** of these graphs might be **different** if they were plotted in **50 years' time**.

....

....

How Motors Work

Q1   **Complete the passage** below using the **words** supplied.

force	angle	stronger	current	magnetic field	permanent magnets

A wire carrying an electric current has a .... around it.

This can interact with the magnetic fields of other wires or of ....

to produce a .... and sometimes movement. A bigger .... or a

.... magnet will produce a bigger force. The size of the force will also depend

on the .... at which the two magnetic fields meet each other.

Q2   The diagram shows a **conducting wire** between two **magnetic poles**. When the current is switched on, the wire **moves** at right angles to the magnetic field.

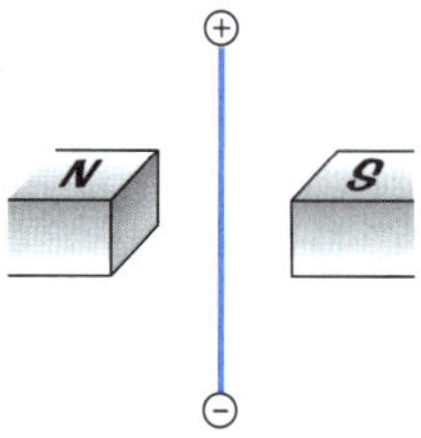

a)   Which way will the wire move? (Hint: use Fleming's left hand rule.)

....

b)   How could the wire be made to move in the **opposite** direction?

....

Q3   Read the three statements below. Tick the box next to each statement that you think is **true**.

☐   A current-carrying wire will not experience a force
if it is **parallel** to the magnetic field of a permanent magnet.

☐   A current-carrying wire will not experience a force
if it is **at right-angles** to the magnetic field of a permanent magnet.

☐   A current-carrying wire will not experience a force if it is
at an **angle of 45°** to the magnetic field of a permanent magnet.

Q4   Read the three statements below. Tick the box next to each statement that you think is **true**.

☐   The split-ring commutator makes the motor spin faster.

☐   The split-ring commutator reverses the direction of the current every half turn by
swapping the contacts to the DC supply.

☐   The split-ring commutator makes the motor rotate in a different direction.

Q5   List four changes that you could make to **speed up** an electric motor.

....

....

....

Power and Efficiency

Q1 Tick the boxes to show whether these statements are **true** or **false**.

True False

a) The total energy supplied to a machine is called the **total energy input**. ☐ ☐

b) The **useful energy output** of a machine is never more than its total energy input. ☐ ☐

c) The **wasted energy** from a machine is the energy it delivers that's not useful. ☐ ☐

d) The more **efficient** a machine is, the more energy it **wastes**. ☐ ☐

Q2 a) Draw lines to match each machine with its **useful energy change**.

Machines:

car

television

light bulb

solar cell

battery

Energy changes:

light ⟹ electrical

electrical ⟹ light

chemical ⟹ kinetic

chemical ⟹ electrical

electrical ⟹ light and sound

b) All machines **waste** some energy. In **what form** is energy most **often** wasted?

....

Q3 **Fill in the gaps** using the **words in the box**. You might need to use some of the words more than once, or not at all.

| power | current |
| what | how long | voltage |

The total energy transferred by an appliance depends on .... it's used

for and its .... rating. The power of an appliance can be calculated

using the formula: power = ... × ....

Q4 Two filament lamps are plugged into a mains supply of **230 volts**.
Lamp A draws a current of **0.43 amps** and **Lamp B** draws a current of **0.17 amps**.

a) What is the power of each lamp?

Lamp A: ....

Lamp B: ....

b) Which lamp is likely to be brighter? ....

Q5 A microwave oven has a power rating of **1 kW**. It is plugged into a **230 volt** mains supply.

Fuses should have a rating that is **slightly higher** than the current flowing.
Which of the following fuses should be used with the microwave oven?
Circle the correct letter A-D.

A 1 A **B** 3 A **C** 5 A **D** 13 A

Be careful — look at the <u>unit</u> that the power rating is given in.

Energy & Efficiency

Q1   Match up the quantities used for calculating electricity costs with the correct units.

The **power** of an electrical appliance.

The **time** an appliance is used for.

The **price** of electrical energy.

The **electrical energy** used by an appliance.

pence per kilowatt-hour

kilowatt-hour (kWh)

hour (h)

kilowatt (kW)

Q2   All the units in the list below are units of **energy**, except for one.

kilojoule   kilowatt   kilowatt-hour   kWh   J

a)   Circle the 'odd one out'.

b)   What **is** this a unit of?   ....

Q3   The amount of energy an appliance uses depends on its **power** and the **time** it's used for.

a)   Calculate how many **kilowatt-hours** of electrical energy a **2 kW** electric heater uses in 3 hours.

Energy used (kWh)   =   power (kW)   ×   time taken (hours)

=   ....   ×   ....

=   .... kWh

b)   Boris gets his electricity supply from Ivasparkco. They charge 7 pence per kilowatt-hour.
Work out the cost of the energy calculated in part (a)

Cost of energy   =   price of one kWh   ×   number of kWh

=   ....   ×   ....

=   .... pence

Energy & Efficiency

Q4   Use the **efficiency formula** to complete the table.

Total Energy Input (J)	Useful Energy Output (J)	Efficiency
2000	1500	
	2000	0.50
4000		0.25
600	200	

Q5   Sajid hopes his new MP3 player is better than his old one. He decides to test which one is more **efficient**.

He puts **identical new batteries** in both MP3 players and switches them on. Then he **times** how long they each play for before the batteries run out.

a)   Why does Sajid use **new** batteries?

....

b)   How can he measure the **useful energy outputs**?

....

c)   Write down one thing Sajid must do to make it a **fair test**.

....

d)   Player A lasts for 3 hours and Player B lasts for 4 hours. Write a **conclusion** for Sajid's experiment.

....

Q6   Tina was investigating a model **winch** — a machine that uses an electric motor to lift objects.

Tina calculated that, in theory, **10 J** of electrical energy would be needed to lift a **boot** 50 cm off a table. She then tried lifting the boot with the winch, and found that, actually, **20 J** of electrical energy was used.

Why did the winch use so much electrical energy in practice?
In your answer, include an explanation of what happened to the 'extra' 10 joules.

....

....

Top Tips: Make sure you use the right formulae for energy, cost and energy efficiency.
Remember to use the correct units for the cost formula — or you'll get the wrong answer.

Energy Efficiency & Cost-Effectiveness

Q1   Heat is lost from a house through its **roof**, **walls**, **doors** and **windows**.

through the roof

....

....

through the walls

....

through the doors

....

....

....

a)   In the spaces on the diagram, write down at least one measure that could be taken to reduce heat losses through each part of the house.

b)   Miss Golightly has just bought a new house which has very large windows. Suggest three ways she could reduce heat loss through the windows of her new house.

....

....

....

Q2   Dr Zarkov is investigating whether **thick curtains** or **draught-proofed windows** are the most **cost-effective**. He knows the initial costs of both, but needs to find which is better at **saving energy**.

a)   He sets up **two sheds** outside his lab, one with thick curtains and one with draught-proofing. He heats both to the **same temperature** and measures how much **energy** it takes to keep each shed at that temperature for two weeks. Give two factors that need to be kept constant for both sheds.

....

....

b)   The shed with curtains uses **16 kWh** over two weeks. The draught-proofed shed uses **17 kWh**. If one kilowatt-hour costs **11 pence**, how much has each shed cost to heat?

Thick curtains: ....

Draught-proofing: ....

Top Tips: If you want to build a new house, there are regulations about making it energy efficient. If you live in an old house, you can sometimes get a grant to cover the cost of insulation.

Energy Efficiency & Cost-Effectiveness

Q3 Mr Tarantino wants to buy **double glazing** for his house, but the salesman tries to sell him insulated window shutters instead. He says they are cheaper and more **cost-effective**.

	Double glazing	Insulated window shutters
Initial Cost	£3000	£1200
Annual Saving	£60	£20
Payback time	50 years	

a) Calculate the **payback time** for insulated shutters and write it in the table.

b) Is the salesman's advice correct? Give reasons for your answer.

....

....

Q4 Two **washing machines** are on sale with the following labels.

Techno A-rated
Power: 2 kW
Average time of cycle: 30 mins
Energy efficiency rating: A
Price: £420

Sudso 2000 Under £400
Power: 2 kW
Average time of cycle: 45 mins
Energy efficiency rating: C
Price: £380

a) i) What is the energy consumption (in kWh) for each cycle for **Techno**?

....

ii) What is the energy consumption (in kWh) for each cycle for **Sudso**?

....

b) The Adejonwo family does **four cycles** of washing each **week**.

i) How much **energy** would they save in **one year** by using Techno instead of Sudso? Give your answer in kilowatt-hours (kWh).

....

ii) 1 kilowatt-hour costs 8p. How much **money** would the family save in one year by using the more expensive machine?

....

iii) What is the **payback time** for buying the more expensive machine?

....

iv) If the Adejonwo family's washing machine lasts 6 years, would it have been **cost-effective** to buy the Techno? Explain your answer.

....

Electrical Safety Devices

Q1 Put **ticks** in the table to show which wires match each description.

Description	Live	Neutral	Earth
Must always be connected			
Just for safety			
Electricity normally flows in and out of it			
Alternates between +ve and –ve voltage			

Morris thought it best to be earthed at all times — just in case.

Q2 **Match** up the beginnings and endings of these sentences:

The live and neutral wires...

A Residual Current Circuit Breaker...

Any metal casing...

... should be connected to the earth wire.

... should normally carry the same current.

... can be used instead of a fuse and earth wire.

Q3 Tick the boxes to show whether these statements are **true** or **false**.

True False

a) The **earth** wire in an electrical cable carries the same current as the **live** and **neutral** wires. ☐ ☐

b) **Neutral** wires are often connected to cold water pipes in the home. ☐ ☐

c) Fuses are placed in the **live** wire of the cable. ☐ ☐

Q4 These sentences describe how a **fuse** and **earth wire** work together to prevent you getting an electric shock from your toaster. Put numbers in the table to show the order they should go in.

	The surge in current causes the fuse wire to heat up.
	Everything is now safe.
	A fault develops and the earthed casing becomes connected to the live supply.
	The live supply is cut off.
	The fuse melts.
	A large current now flows in through the live wire and out through the earth wire.

Q5 **Residual Current Circuit Breakers (RCCBs)** are more **convenient** than fuses because they can be **reset** rather than having to be **replaced** (like a fuse).

a) What has to happen for an **RCCB** to detect a fault in the circuit?

....

b) Why does an **RCCB** offer you **better protection** from electrocution than a fuse?

....

....

Energy from New Technology

Q1 Give one advantage and one disadvantage of using **solar cells** to generate electricity.

Advantage: ....

Disadvantage: ....

Q2 One **solar panel** receives **1.5 kW** of power from the Sun. The panel is **15% efficient**.

a) How many of these panels would be needed to power a **4.5 kW** appliance?

....

....

b) Why might people **not want** to use these panels?

....

c) On a cloudy day the sunlight on each panel could drop to **0.5 kW**.
How much power could the same group of panels then provide?

....

d) Why are solar panels a better energy resource in **Southern Italy** than they are in **Southern Ireland**?

....

Q3 Answer these questions about **potential new alternatives** to the **National Grid**.

a) Give **three problems** associated with transmitting electricity through the **National Grid**.

1. ....

2. ....

3. ....

b) **i)** Why would **solar panels** on a **satellite** be more reliable than those on **rooftops** on Earth?

....

ii) How could we get energy from these solar panels on satellites **to Earth**, to use in our homes?

....

c) **i)** Why would transmission cables made of a **superconducting** material not have any power loss?

....

ii) Why don't we use superconducting cables already?

....

Energy from New Technology

Q4   People often **object** to **wind turbines** being put up near to where they live.

   a)   Give two reasons why they might **object**.

....

....

....

   b)   List three arguments **in favour** of using wind turbines to generate electricity.

     1. ....

     2. ....

     3. ....

Q5   Choose the **best renewable** option from the list below for each of the given **situations**.
Give a **reason** for each choice that you make.

> **Renewable options**: geothermal, biomass, wave converters, wind turbines, hydroelectric.

   a)   Situation 1: a small **flat** island in the middle of an ocean, with **little wind** and a **low rainfall**.

     Choice .... Reason ....

     ....

   b)   Situation 2: a **hilly** area with **low rainfall**.

     Choice .... Reason ....

     ....

   c)   Situation 3: a **hilly** area with **high rainfall**.

     Choice .... Reason ....

     ....

   d)   Situation 4: An area with **hot water geysers**.

     Choice .... Reason ....

     ....

Energy from New Technology

Q6 Tick the boxes to show whether these statements are **true** or **false**.

		True	False
a)	Biomass can only be obtained from dead animals and plants.	☐	☐
b)	Solar panels can only work where it is constantly sunny.	☐	☐
c)	Tidal barrages could affect fish migration.	☐	☐
d)	Renewables cause less pollution than fossil fuels.	☐	☐
e)	Wind turbines can only be sited on hilltops.	☐	☐

Q7 Draw lines to match up each **medical device** with the **condition it treats** and the **way it works**.

pacemaker   Parkinson's disease   small electrical impulses

defibrillator   severe depression   nerve stimulation

deep brain stimulator   lack of heart beat   electric shock

electroconvulsive therapy   irregular heartbeat   current through the brain

Q8 An **old advertisement** states that wearing an electrical bracelet will cure blisters.

Bob the scientist takes **20 people with blisters** and fits **10** of them with an **electrical bracelet** and **10** with bracelets that have **no electrical connection**. After one week **8 people** wearing the **electrical** bracelets and **6 people** wearing the **other bracelets** had their blisters **cured**.

a) How reliable do you think Bob's results are? Explain your answer.

....

b) How could he improve the experiment?

....

c) Why did he include the 10 people with bracelets that were **not electrical**?

....

d) Why did he wait for a week before examining all the people tested?

....

e) Explain how the results **support the advertisement** or **fail to support the advertisement**.

....

....

Mixed Questions — P1a Topics 9 & 10

Q1 Dr Fergals has developed a new type of lagging, material X, for **insulating** hot water tanks.

a) How could Dr Fergals test whether material X is **cost-effective** compared with fibreglass wool?

....

....

b) i) Dr Fergals tests the new type of lagging. Complete the table below to find
out which material is more cost-effective. Electricity costs **14 pence per kWh**.

Type of lagging	Energy used in 1 week (kWh)	Cost per year (£)	Saving per year (£)	Initial cost (£)	Payback time (years)
None	10		-	0	-
Fibreglass wool	8			60	
Material X	6			100	

ii) Which material is the most cost-effective? ....

Q2 The diagram shows a **generator** that is turned by a wind turbine.

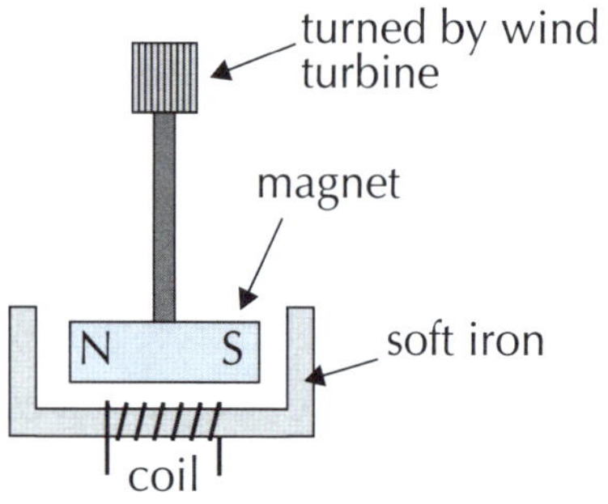

a) What happens in the coil of wire when the magnet is rotated
at a constant speed? Explain your answer.

....

....

turned by wind turbine

magnet

N   S

soft iron

coil

b) The generator is attached to a cathode ray oscilloscope (CRO).

A

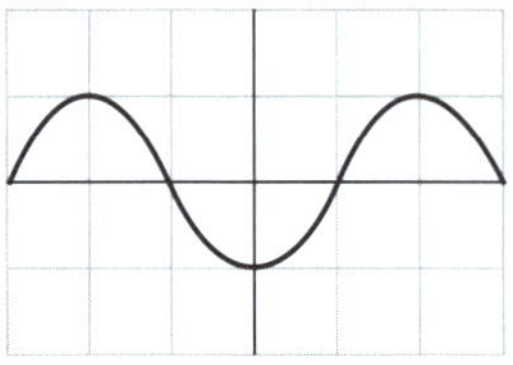

B

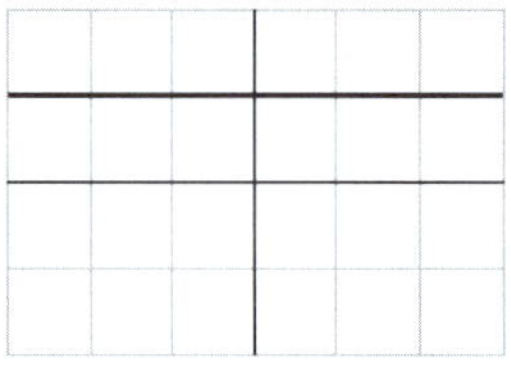

i) Circle the letter of the diagram that
could show the output of the generator.

ii) Suggest a source for the other diagram.

....

iii) How would the CRO trace change if the magnet was rotated **twice as fast**?

....

c) Give one advantage and one disadvantage of using wind power to source all the UK's electricity.

....

....

d) Electricity is transmitted by the National Grid. Suggest an alternative that could improve efficiency.

....

e) Give two methods of **communication** that would not be possible without electricity.

....

Mixed Questions — P1a Topics 9 & 10

Q3 When Mike goes potholing, he wears a **torch** on his helmet so he can see where he is going.

Mike has been using a **3 V** dry-cell battery with a stated capacity of **20 A h**.

a) For how long can it supply a current of **250 mA**?

....

b) Mike investigates batteries with different voltages by measuring the current in the torch circuit.

i) State the equation relating voltage and current. ....

ii) Mike plots a graph of his data. It has a **curved** shape. What caused this to happen?

....

c) Pete, Mike's friend powers his torch using a **solar cell**. Pete uses a datalogger to record the amount of sunlight available while the battery charges.

Give one advantage of using a **datalogging** system to record data.

....

d) After charging, Pete switches his torch on. The bulb goes off after **1980 s**.
The power rating of Pete's torch is 300 mW.

i) Complete the table to calculate the combined efficiency of the torch and solar cell.

Energy input	Useful energy output	Efficiency
4200 J		

ii) Give one reason why solar cells are not in widespread use.

....

Q4 The diagram below shows a simple **motor** from a hairdryer. The coil is rotating as shown.

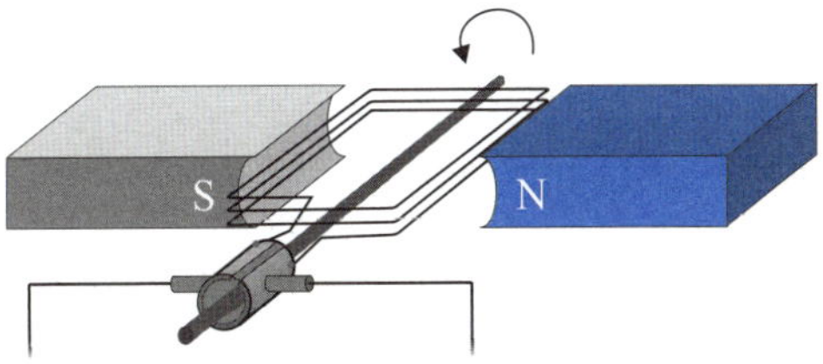

a) On the diagram, draw arrows labelled 'F' to show the direction of the **force** on each arm of the coil.

b) Draw arrows labelled 'I' on each arm of the coil to show the direction the **current** is flowing.

The electricity supply is at **230 V** and the power rating of the hairdryer is **350 W**.

c) **i)** What does electrical power measure? ....

ii) Calculate the current the hairdryer draws. ....

d) The **temperature** of the hairdryer must be kept within certain limits. What component could be used to automatically control the heater within the hairdryer? ....

e) The hairdryer uses a residual current circuit breaker. What advantage does this have over a fuse?

....

Use of Waves in Scanning

Q1   Choose from the words below to complete this passage.

lead	plastic	bones	transmitted	soft tissue	aluminium	absorbed

X-rays can pass easily through .... but are ....

more by .... Screens and shields made of

.... are used to minimise unnecessary exposure to X-rays.

Q2   Indicate whether the following statements about X-rays are **true** or **false**.

True   **False**

a)   X-ray photographs show "shadows of our bones".   ☐ ☐

b)   Flesh is more dense than bone so it lets X-rays through more easily.   ☐ ☐

c)   Radiographers wear lead aprons to protect their clothing.   ☐ ☐

d)   X-rays don't easily pass through bones because they are absorbed by them.   ☐ ☐

Q3   Use the words in the box to **complete the paragraph** about **infrared** radiation.

bright	dark	electrical	heat	hot	night-vision

Infrared is another name for .... radiation. People give out infrared

because they are .... The police use ....

equipment to let them see people in the .... The equipment changes

infrared into an .... signal which then appears as a

.... spot on a screen.

Q4   **Draw lines** to match the waves to their **uses**.

microwaves

X-rays

ultraviolet

visible

to detect forged bank notes

to measure cloud patterns

to examine **X-ray** photographs

to detect fractures in bones

Q5   Which of the following works by wave **reflection**? Circle the correct letter(s) A-D.

A prenatal scanning

B X-rays

C night-vision camera

D reading a book

Use of Waves in Scanning

Q6 For each of these questions on **iris scanning**, tick the appropriate box.

a) What is **biometrics**?
- [ ] The use of cosmetics to change your eye colour.
- [ ] The use of automated measurements taken from your body.
- [ ] The study of easily recognised patterns.

b) How is **iris data** obtained?
- [ ] It is entered into a computer.
- [ ] It is translated into a code.
- [ ] It is photographed with a camera.

c) What makes iris data good for **security checks**?
- [ ] Everybody has a unique pattern.
- [ ] It works in low-intensity light.
- [ ] It is totally foolproof.

Q7 **Ultrasound scanning** can reveal things about a **developing foetus**.

a) For prenatal scanning, why is it **better** to use **ultrasound** than **X-rays**?

....

....

b) Why might parents **want** to scan their unborn child?

....

....

c) What **ethical difficulties** might the parents then have to face?

....

....

....

Top Tips: It's not enough just to know how ultrasound scanning can be used to produce images of a foetus — you also need to consider the ethical issues involved. It's a good idea to have a think about these now so that you'll know what the arguments are when it comes to the exam.

Use of Waves in Scanning

Q8   Ultraviolet radiation is useful in detecting bank note forgeries.

a)   What does a **fluorescent** material do when exposed to ultraviolet radiation?

....

....

b)   Explain how banks can detect forgeries using **fluorescent ink** on their banknotes.

....

....

....

Q9   This diagram represents a **rainfall radar** picture of part of Britain, made using microwaves.

a)   **Where** would the microwaves be emitted from?

....

....

b)   What happens to the microwaves that are **not reflected back** to make the picture?

....

c)   i)   In which of the places shown is it likely to have been **raining** when the picture was taken?

....

   ii)   How can you **tell**?

....

d)   Why can **cosmic microwaves** not be used to tell where it's raining?

....

e)   Describe how cosmic microwaves can be used in weather forecasting.

....

....

Top Tip: As I'm sure you well know there are loads of different practical uses of waves. Make sure you know them and any limitations they might have — it could just pop up on the exam.

Waves — Basic Principles

Q1 Diagrams A, B and C represent **electromagnetic waves**.

A **B** **C**

a) Which two diagrams show waves with the same **frequency**? ...... and ......

b) Which two diagrams show waves with the same **amplitude**? ...... and ......

c) Which two diagrams show waves with the same **wavelength**? ...... and ......

Q2 A ripple in a pond travels at **0.5 m/s**. It makes a duck bob up and down **twice every second**.

a) What is the **frequency** of the duck's bobbing? ....

Remember what's meant by a wavelength, then use $v = f\lambda$.

b) When the duck is on the crest of a wave, **how far away** is the next crest?

....

Q3 **Green light** travels at 3×10^8 m/s and has a wavelength of about 5×10^{-7} m.

Calculate the **frequency** of green light. Give the correct unit in your answer.

You'll have to use $v = f\lambda$.

....

....

Q4 The graph is a **CRO** representation of a **sound wave**.

a) What is the **amplitude** of the wave on the CRO screen?

....

b) How many **complete** vibrations are shown? ....

c) **How long** does it take to make each vibration? ....

Q5 Put the following frequencies in order of **size**, from the **highest** frequency to the **lowest** frequency.

90 MHz   **900 kHz**   **9 000 000 Hz**   **9 × 10⁴ Hz**   **9 × 10² MHz**

It'll help if you put them all into hertz, and in standard form.

....

More Waves — Principles

Q1   Here are **two ways** in which you can make waves on a **slinky** spring.

①   ②

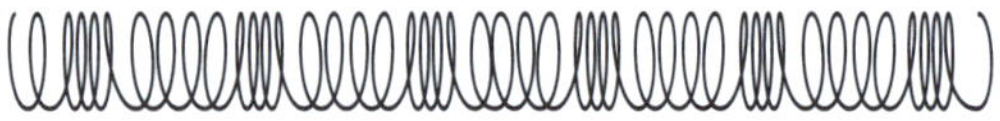

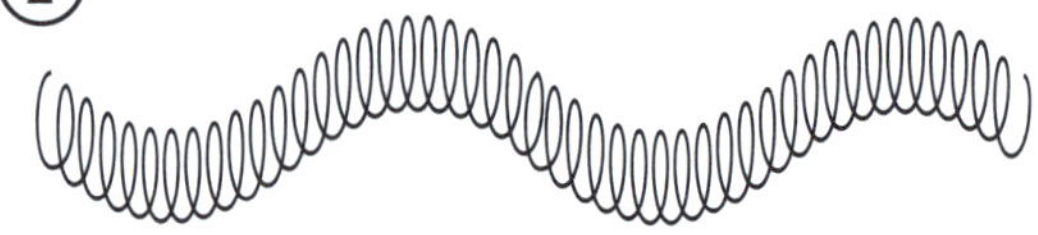

Which diagram shows a **transverse** wave, and which one shows a **longitudinal** wave?

Transverse: ....   Longitudinal: ....

Q2   Sort the waves below into two groups — **longitudinal** waves and **transverse** waves.

sunlight   'push-pull' wave on a slinky   ultraviolet   'shake' wave on a slinky

ultrasound   microwaves   birdsong   drumbeat

Longitudinal: ....

Transverse: ....

Q3   Sound waves are **longitudinal** waves.

a)   Which **direction** are the vibrations in a longitudinal wave,
compared to the direction the wave is **travelling**? ....

b)   What is meant by the **frequency** of a longitudinal / sound wave?

....

c)   As sound waves travel through a material they produce compressions and rarefactions.

   i) What are **compressions**? ....

....

   ii) What are **rarefactions**? ....

....

Q4   Circle the letters to show which of the following statements about waves are **true**.

A Absorption of waves can increase the temperature of objects.

B Transverse waves are all electromagnetic.

C Longitudinal waves cannot be displayed on a CRO.

D A compression happens when the medium is squashed.

Reflection of Waves

Q1   A boat is sending pulses of **ultrasound** down to the seabed and then receiving the reflection. The sea is **750 m deep** where the boat is, and it takes **1 second** to receive the echo.

a)   How **fast** does the ultrasound travel in the sea water?   Use speed = distance / time

....

b)   If the boat passes over a **wreck**, what will happen to the time taken to receive the echo?

....

Q2   Use these words to complete the passage.

boundary   density   images   medium   reflected

When a wave goes from one .... to another, some of

its energy is .... at the .... between

them. This allows us to see .... in transparent objects.

This partial reflection can be caused by changes in ....

Q3   Astronauts who visited the Moon left a **mirror** on its surface. A pulse of laser light is sent from Earth to hit the mirror. The laser light is received back on Earth **2.5 seconds later**.

a)   Light travels at **3 × 10^8 m/s**. How **far away** is the Moon?   Think about the path the light takes...

....

b)   Why could the measurement **not** be carried out using **ultrasound**?

....

Q4   A boy stands **165 m** away from the wall of a football stadium. He claps his hands and listens for the echo. When he claps at a rate of **60 claps per minute**, each **echo** coincides with the **next clap**.

a)   What **speed of sound** does his result suggest? ....

b)   Why doesn't he just time the echo of a single clap?

....

c)   If he wants the clapping rate to **decrease** should he move **nearer** to or **further** from the wall? Explain your answer.

....

....

Refraction of Waves

Q1 What causes **light** to be **refracted**? Tick the correct box.

☐ Refraction is caused by an image being formed at the boundary between two media.

☐ Refraction is caused by light being reflected off the boundary between two media.

☐ Refraction is caused by one medium being better able to absorb light than another.

☐ Refraction is caused by light changing speed as it enters another medium.

Q2 Jo is looking at a pebble lying on the bottom of a **pool**.

a) Does the bottom of the pool appear to be **nearer** to Jo
or **further away** from her than it actually is?

....

b) Does light travel **faster** or **more slowly** in air than in water?

....

Q3 The diagram shows a light ray
passing through **air** and through **glass**.

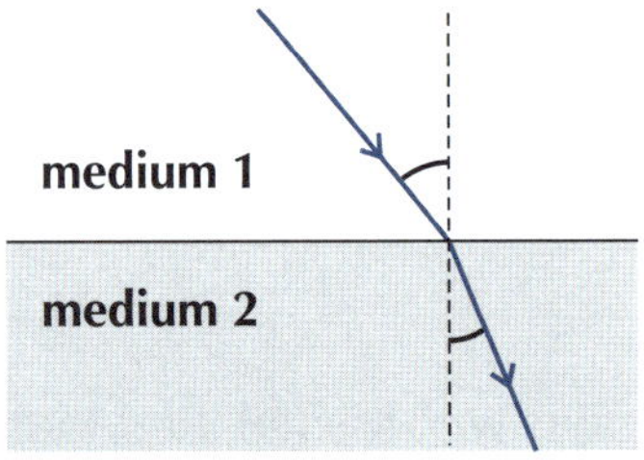

medium 1

medium 2

a) Fill in the gaps in this sentence to say
which medium is **air** and which is **glass**.

Medium 1 in the diagram is .... and **medium 2** is ....

b) **Explain** your answer to part a).

....

c) Would your answer to a) be the **same** if the wave was a **sound wave**? Explain why.

....

Q4 The diagram below shows rays of light entering three **glass prisms**.
For each prism **sketch the path** the ray takes as it passes through the prism.

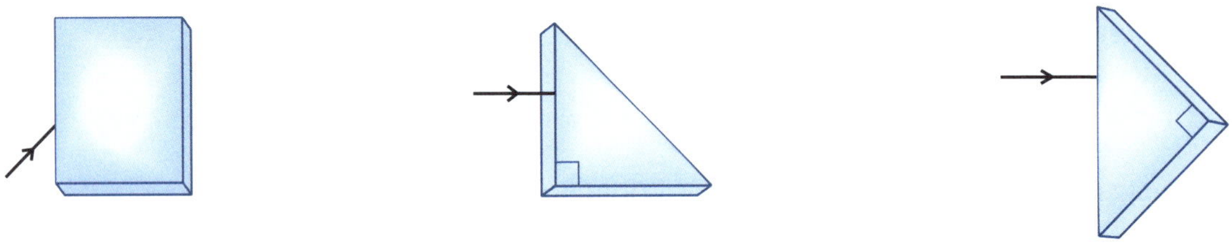

It helps to sketch in the <u>normal</u> to each boundary. Then you can see
more clearly whether the ray is refracted <u>towards</u> it or <u>away</u>.

Electromagnetic Waves

Q1   Tick the boxes to show whether the following statements are **true** or **false**.

True False

a)   Visible light travels faster in a vacuum than both X-rays and radio waves.   ☐ ☐

b)   All EM waves transfer matter from place to place.   ☐ ☐

c)   Radio waves have the shortest wavelength of all EM waves.   ☐ ☐

d)   All EM waves can travel through space.   ☐ ☐

Q2   Red and violet are at opposite ends of the spectrum of **visible** light.
Describe two things they have in **common** and two ways in which they **differ**.

Similarities ....

....

Differences ....

....

Q3   The graph opposite shows how the **energy** of EM waves varies with **frequency**.

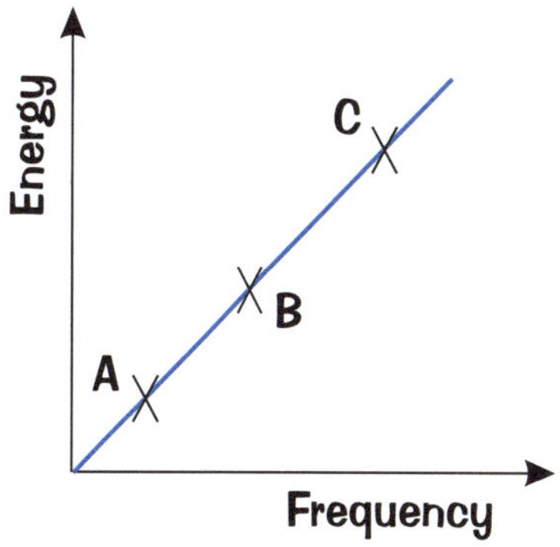

a)   What is the mathematical relationship between frequency and energy?

....

....

b)   Draw **arrows** to match points **A**, **B** and **C** from the graph to the **three types of radiation** below.

| green light | gamma radiation | radio waves |

☐A   ☐B   ☐C

Q4   EM waves with higher frequencies are generally more damaging.

a)   Explain, in terms of wavelength and frequency, why some **ultraviolet** radiation can be almost as damaging as **X-rays**.

....

....

b)   Give two effects that EM waves can have when they are **absorbed by matter**.

1. ....

2. ....

Electromagnetic Waves

Q5 Explain **why**:

a) Excessive **sunbathing** can be dangerous.

....

....

....

b) **Darker-skinned** people are **less likely** to suffer from skin cancer.

....

....

Q6 Here are four different types of **electromagnetic wave**:

| ultraviolet | microwaves | X-rays | infrared |

a) Which has the **lowest frequency**? ....

b) Which carries the **most energy**? ....

c) Which can cause damage by **ionisation**? ....

Q7 It has been suggested that using **mobile phones** could cause **brain tumours**. However, at the moment there is **no reliable evidence** to prove that this is or isn't the case.

a) What could happen to the **brains** of people who use mobile phones?

....

b) Why do people still **take the risk** by using mobile phones?

....

c) Why might scientists find it difficult to get **reliable evidence** about the risks of using mobile phones?

....

....

Top Tips: Scientists have to weigh up evidence when deciding how risky an activity is — and the more evidence they have, the more confident they can be in their predictions. We already know enough about EM waves in general to be able to say which ones cause the most damage to the body.

Seismic Waves

Q1 The diagram shows the **structure** of the **Earth**.

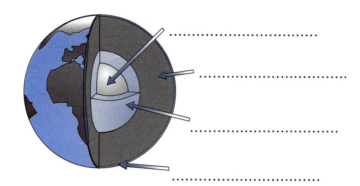

....

....

....

....

Add these labels to the correct places on the diagram.

| crust | mantle | inner core | outer core |

Q2 **Draw lines** to match each of these words with the **correct definition**. One has been done for you.

seismic waves

seismograph

P-waves

S-waves

outer core

inner core

refraction

solid part of the Earth's core

shock waves from an earthquake

liquid part of the Earth's core

longitudinal seismic waves

a device that records seismic waves

change of direction caused by a change in speed

seismic waves that cannot travel through liquids

Q3 Which of the following can **not** be used to predict earthquakes?
Circle the correct letter(s):

A Dogs barking more than usual.

B Birds flying inland.

C The history of the frequency of earthquakes.

D A decrease in tourist numbers.

E Groundwater levels.

F An increase in radioactive gas emission from rocks.

Seismic Waves

Q4 When there's an earthquake, **seismic waves** travel through the Earth.
Two types of seismic wave are S-waves and P-waves.

a) Why do both S and P waves **curve** as they travel through the Earth's mantle?

....

b) Why do seismic waves abruptly change direction about halfway through the Earth?

....

c) Why are S-waves **not** detected at the Earth's surface immediately opposite the
site of the earthquake?

....

d) What evidence do we have that the **inner core** of the Earth is solid?

....

e) What evidence is there that the **mantle** is also solid?

....

Q5 This is a **seismogram** showing the arrival of
an **S-wave** and a **P-wave** after an earthquake.

a) Why do the two traces **not** arrive **together**?

....

b) Which trace shows the arrival of the P-wave — A or B?   ....

c) The average speed of the P-waves is **12 000 m/s** through the mantle.
Approximately how far was the seismograph from the site of the earthquake?

....

....

d) Describe three ways in which a seismogram recorded immediately opposite the site of the
earthquake would be **different** from the one shown above.

1. ....

2. ....

3. ....

Digital Technology

Q1   **Fill in the blanks**, using the words below.

analogue	digital	amplified	weaken	interference	noise

All signals .... as they travel. To overcome this, they can be

.... Signals may also suffer .... from

other signals or from electrical disturbances. This causes ....

in the signal. When .... signals are amplified, the noise is

also amplified.

Q2   Signals can either be **analogue** or **digital**, and both can pick up noise as they travel.

a)   Sketch: a 'clean' digital signal   a 'noisy' digital signal   a 'noisy' analogue signal.

b)   Explain why digital signals suffer less from **noise** than analogue signals.

....

....

c)   State one other **advantage** of using digital signals for communication.

....

Q3   Digital technology has had a big impact on the **music industry**.

a)   Give **two** examples of ways in which digital technology has
changed the way music is **stored**.

....

....

b)   What new sorts of **musical instruments** have been produced as a result of digital technology?

....

Digital Technology

Q4 A **cable TV** company sends TV signals to houses along **optical fibres**.

a) What type(s) of **EM waves** could be used to send the signals along the optical fibres?

....

b) Give **three advantages** of using optical fibres to transmit signals, rather than **broadcasting** them (sending them through the air from a large transmitter on a hilltop, say).

1. ....

2. ....

3. ....

Q5 Doctors can use **optical fibres** to look inside a patient's body during **keyhole surgery**. One bundle of fibres is used to carry light into the body, and another to return the reflected light back to a monitor.

a) What kind of **material** could the optical fibres be made from?

....

b) Optical fibres work because of **total internal reflection** within the fibre. If there **wasn't** total internal reflection inside the fibre, **what would happen** to the signal sent down the fibre?

....

c) On this diagram, draw lines to show the path that a ray transmitting a signal could take.

Top Tips: Luckily you **don't** need to know the **gory details** of how total internal reflection works for this module. You just need to know that it happens, and what **optical fibres** are used for.

The Solar System

Q1   Use the words in the box to **complete the paragraph**.

asteroid belt	inner	Saturn	Jupiter	Mars	moons	Solar System	asteroid

Our .... is made up of the Sun and its surrounding

planets. The four planets closest to the Sun are known as the ....

planets while the rest of the planets are called the outer planets. Between these two

types of planet there is also an ....

Some of the planets are orbited by natural satellites called ....

Q2   Even though the Earth's radius is a massive 6378 km, it's very small compared to the scale of the Universe.

a)   Rearrange the following list of **astronomical things** into size order, starting with the smallest.

galaxy   moon   star   planet   Universe

.... ➡ .... ➡ .... ➡ .... ➡ ....

b)   Fill in the table of **astronomical distances** with the **numbers 1-4**, to put them into the **correct order of size**. Make the smallest distance number 1 and the largest distance number 4.

	Distance between Earth and Sun
	Distance between stars
	Distance between galaxies
	Distance between Earth and Moon

Q3   Which one of the following statements is **not true**?
Tick the appropriate box.

☐   A galaxy is made up of millions (or even billions) of stars.

☐   The distance between galaxies can be millions of times the distance between stars.

☐   Gravity is the force which keeps stars apart.

☐   Galaxies rotate in space.

The Solar System

Q4 Draw lines to join up each **central box** with correct descriptions from the boxes on the right and left.

| They are usually smaller than planets. | **STARS** | They can be seen because of reflected light. |

| Billions of these make up the Milky Way. | **PLANETS** | They orbit planets. |

| They give out light and heat. | **MOONS** | They orbit stars. |

Q5 Tick the correct box to show whether each of these statements is **true** or **false**.

		true	false
a)	Mercury is the nearest planet to the Sun.	☐	☐
b)	Planets orbit the Sun in perfect circular orbits	☐	☐
c)	The stars in galaxies move as the galaxy slowly rotates	☐	☐
d)	The Sun is at the centre of the Milky Way galaxy	☐	☐

Q6 A typical modern space explorer craft can travel at **17 kilometres a second**.

a) Use this information to **complete the table** below

	Distance from Earth / km	Time for an explorer craft to reach here / seconds
Jupiter	630 000 000	
Pluto		282 000 000
Our nearest star	39 900 000 000 000	

b) Approximately how many **years** would it take to reach our nearest star?

....

c) Why would it be **difficult to communicate** with a spacecraft halfway to Jupiter?

....

....

Top Tips: As **Douglas Adams** wrote in the *Hitchhiker's Guide to the Galaxy*, "Space is **big**. You just won't believe how vastly, hugely, **mind-bogglingly big** it is. I mean, you may think it's a long way down the road to the chemist's, but that's just **peanuts** to space." And he was **not wrong**.

The Universe

Q1   Read the following passage and **underline the correct word or words** in each pair.

Comets are balls of ice and dust that orbit the Sun in circular / **elongated elliptical** orbits. They often orbit in **the same plane as** / **a different plane from** the planets. When comets approach the Sun they **speed up** / **slow down** because the Sun's gravity has **more** / **less** of an effect. If a comet passes close to Earth's orbit it is known as a Near Earth Object, or NEO.

Q2   Almost all asteroids in the Solar System lie in the **asteroid belt**.

a)   Where in the Solar System would you find the asteroid belt?

....

b)   What might cause an asteroid to **leave its orbit** and head **towards Earth**?

....

Q3   Write down three ways in which the orbit of a **comet** is different from the orbit of an **asteroid**.

1. ....

2. ....

3. ....

Q4   Tick the correct box to show whether each of these statements is **true** or **false**.

		true	false
a)	The Sun is at the centre of a comet's orbit.	☐	☐
b)	Occasionally a meteor will cause damage on Earth.	☐	☐
c)	A comet's tail can only be seen when it is close to the Sun.	☐	☐
d)	A meteor that hits Earth's surface is called a meteorite.	☐	☐

Q5   Astronomers track the trajectories of **NEOs**.

a)   Apart from comets, write down one astronomical object that could be an NEO. ....

b)   Why would we be worried if an NEO was found on a collision course with Earth?

....

....

Hint — what may have happened to the dinosaurs?

Space Flight

Q1 It would be a **very bad idea** to go out into **space** without any **protection**.

    a) Identify **two hazards** associated with **exposure** to the **Sun's rays**.

       1. ....

       2. ....

    b) Why are space suits **pressurised**?

       ....

Q2 Which of the following disorders is not recognised as a potential problem on a long space flight? Circle the correct letter **A-D**.

      A Wasted muscles   **B** Weak bones   **C** Bruising   **D** Psychological problems

Q3 Long space missions carrier a **higher risk** to the astronauts' health than shorter space missions.

    a) Why would the Sun's radiation cause **more** problems on a mission to **Mars** than one to the **Moon**?

       ....

    b) Why are long space missions bad for the **heart**?

       ....

       ....

Q4 Scientists carefully plan how to **limit** the bad effects of space on astronauts.

    a) Draw lines to join up each **effect of space flight** with the **on-board solution** designed to minimise the problem.

       weak muscles   exercise bikes

       weak heart   radiation shields

       bone wastage   artificial gravity

       skin cancer   special diet

Over-exposure to the Sun's radiation can cause skin cancer.

    b) How could a spacecraft generate **artificial gravity**?

       ....

Q5 Write down two reasons why space flight can cause **psychological stress** (as well as physical problems).

       ....

       ....

Forces, Energy and Space Flight

Q1   Newton's force laws apply in space as well as on Earth.

a)   Fill in the **gaps** in this statement about **forces**.

Each **action** has an .... and .... reaction.

b)   A spacecraft's **rocket engine** burns fuel, producing exhaust gas. **Underline the correct word** in each pair to explain how this makes the spacecraft **move**.

> The exhaust gas is pushed out of the front / back of the spacecraft by the action / reaction force. The spacecraft has a(n) equal / double reaction force pushing it forwards / backwards.

Q2   Two spacecraft have been fitted with the same rocket engine. The first has a mass of 1100 kg and an acceleration of 28.0 m/s². The second only manages an acceleration of 17.1 m/s².

a)   Using the equation **F = ma**, calculate the **force** the engine can exert.

....

b)   What's the **mass** of the second spacecraft to the nearest kg?

....

Q3   A spacecraft is launched into space from the surface of the Earth using a rocket engine.

Describe the **main energy changes** that take place during the launch.

....

....

....

Q4   A spacecraft with mass **5000 kg** is going to land on a planet. It accelerates towards the planet, then as it approaches the planet's surface it slows right down to give itself a gentle landing.

a)   The spacecraft accelerates at **10 m/s²**. Calculate the force acting on the spacecraft.

....

b)   Assuming the planet's atmosphere is thin, is it enough for the spacecraft to **switch off** its rocket engine in order to **slow down**? **Explain** your answer.

....

....

Top Tips: There are **two important things to learn** if you want to get these questions right. The first one is the rule about **action** and **reaction**. The second one's about **F**, **m** and **a**...

Gravity, Mass and Weight

Q1   Which of these statements about **gravity** are **true**? Tick the appropriate boxes.

☐ Gravity is an attractive force between the weights of two objects.

☐ Objects have mass because they have weight.

☐ Objects have weight because they have mass.

☐ The bigger the mass, the stronger its gravity is.

☐ The gravitational pull of a black hole is so strong even light can't escape.

Q2   Two scientists are discussing a trip to **Mars**. They have different points of view.

Professor Brown: "We need less fuel for the return trip — the rocket has less mass on Mars."
Professor White: "We need less fuel for the return trip because the rocket weighs less on Mars."

Who is right, and why is the other wrong? (Ignore the amount of fuel burned getting to Mars.)

....

....

Q3   A space probe lands on the icy surface of **Europa**, a moon of Jupiter. It weighs a set of **known masses**, but the readings are not very accurate. **Plot a graph** on the axes using the information from the table, and use it to **estimate** the **strength of Europa's gravity**.

Mass	Weight
0.1 kg	0.15 N
0.2 kg	0.30 N
0.3 kg	0.36 N
0.4 kg	0.55 N
0.5 kg	0.68 N

Graph of Weight Against Mass

....

....

....

....

Q4   An object weighing **50 N** on Earth is taken to Mars, where it reads **1.9 kg** on a set of Earth scales. Work out the **acceleration due to gravity** on Mars.

First find the Earth mass, then you can find the relationship between the gravity on Earth and Mars.

....

....

....

P1b Topic 12 — Space and Its Mysteries

The Life Cycle of Stars

Q1 Complete the passage, choosing from the words given below.

gravity	millions	hot	fusion	stable	inwards	outwards	billions	fission	mass

When a protostar gets .... enough, hydrogen nuclei will start to undergo

nuclear .... and the star enters its .... phase (becoming a

main sequence star). The force from the heat generated inside the star (pushing

...............................) and the force of gravity (pushing ....) are balanced.

The star might stay in this stable phase for .... of years.

Q2 Describe the difference between a **first generation** star and a **second generation** star.

....

....

Q3 Towards the end of its life, a **main sequence** star will become a **red giant**.

a) What causes a star to become a **red giant**?

....

....

b) Why is a red giant **red**?

....

c) What happens to **small stars** like our Sun after they become red giants?

....

....

Q4 Some red giants start to undergo **more fusion reactions**, glow very brightly and then **explode**.

Give the **name** of this explosion, and describe what happens after it.

....

....

....

....

....

44

The Life Cycle of Stars

Hint — these bodies have undergone periods of intense <u>contraction</u>.

Q5 Neutron stars are made of matter that is very **different** from the matter that planet Earth is made from. What is the **cause** of this difference?

....

....

....

Q6 Below is a diagram showing the **life cycle** of **stars**.

Clouds of Dust and Gas
Red Giant
Neutron Star
Protostar
Black Hole
Main Sequence Star
Black Dwarf
White Dwarf
Supernova

Match the letters to the words on the right of the diagram.

A ....

B ....

C ....

D ....

E ....

F ....

G ....

H ....

I ....

Top Tips: This star life cycle might seem a bit weird and wonderful, but really it's just a **series of events** that you've got to **learn**. If you don't remember which things happen to big stars and which happen to smaller stars (like our Sun) get your books and notes out and **revise** it.

Robots and Remote Sensing

Q1 Scientists use **remote sensing** to investigate other planets.

a) Give the name of one robot lander that has investigated the surface of **Mars**.

....

b) Give an advantage of **remote sensing**, compared to landing a robot on the surface of a planet.

....

c) Give an advantage of **landing a robot** on the **surface** of a planet, compared to remote sensing.

....

Q2 The diagram shows a (made-up) **space probe** called **Erik** orbiting **Titan**, which is one of **Saturn's moons**.

not to scale

Erik

Titan

Saturn

Earth

a) How would Erik **transmit data** back to Earth?

....

b) i) When Erik is in the position shown in the diagram, it **can't transmit data** to Earth. Why not?

....

ii) How could scientists **get around** this problem?

....

....

Q3 Jennifer reads an article which says that scientists have discovered **changes** in the **chemical composition** of a distant planet's atmosphere.

a) Jennifer knows this is related to the search for extraterrestrial life. **Explain how** a change in the composition of a planet's atmosphere could be **evidence** for **life** on that planet.

....

....

b) **What other information** can scientists get from remote sensing to help them search for **life** on a planet?

....

Is there Anybody Out There?

Q1 So far, no evidence of life has been found on the other planets in our Solar System.

  a) Why is there no life on **Neptune**? ....

  b) What is meant by **the Goldilocks zone**?

....

Q2 The diagram shows a **star system** somewhat similar to our Solar System.

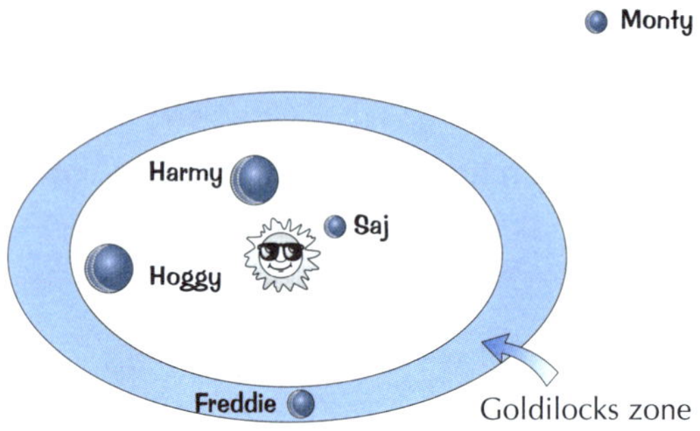

  a) Which planet can **currently** support life?

....

  b) If the star began to **enlarge** (as our Sun will), what **other** planet might **become** life-friendly?

....

Monty

Harmy

Hoggy

Saj

Freddie

Goldilocks zone

Q3 It is possible that there might be life on one of **Jupiter's moons**.

  a) Why is it **extremely unlikely** that there could be **intelligent** life on any of Jupiter's moons?

....

  b) The Sun has had to be in a **stable** phase for intelligent life to evolve on Earth. Why is this?

....

Q4 a) What is the **aim** of the **SETI** project? ....

  b) What **evidence** do scientists on the SETI project look for?

....

  c) How can the **general public** help SETI with this?

....

Q5 Susan says that if **intelligent life** really existed outside Earth, we would have been **contacted** by aliens **before now** — and we **haven't** been contacted, therefore we are **alone** in the Universe.

Give arguments **against** Susan's idea.

....

....

The Origins of the Universe

Q1 **Complete this passage** using the words supplied below.

| expansion | matter | energy | expand | age | explosion |

Many scientists believe that the Universe started with all the

.... and .... in one small space.

There was a huge .... and space and the material in it started

to .... Scientists can estimate the .... of

the Universe using the current rate of ....

Q2 The '**Big Bang**' and '**Steady State**' theories are two theories of the origin of the Universe.

a) Briefly explain the idea behind the Steady State theory.

....

....

b) What does this theory suggest is happening as the Universe is expanding?

....

Q3 What **evidence** is there to support the idea that the Universe is expanding?
Include a brief explanation of **red-shift** in your answer.

....

....

....

....

Q4 The **expanding universe** can be likened to the surface of a **bubble** which is **getting bigger**.

a) What happens to two "particles" which start off **next** to each other as the bubble **expands**?

....

b) Why do astronomers want to know how fast the expansion of the Universe is slowing down (or not)?

....

c) If there was no gravity, what would happen to the expansion rate of the Universe?

....

The Future of the Universe

Q1   The Universe will either **stop expanding** and **eventually contract**
until there's a "Big Crunch" or it will **keep expanding forever**.

Write down two factors that will influence the eventual fate of the Universe.

1. ....

2. ....

Q2   As well as normal matter, the Universe also contains **dark matter**.

a)   How is **dark matter** different from "normal" matter?

....

b)   Could some of the dark matter be in black holes and dust clouds? ....

c)   Is all of the dark matter in black holes and dust clouds? ....

Q3   **Number** these statements to show the **order of events** in the **Oscillating Universe Theory**.

	Gravity stops the Universe expanding.		The next Big Bang happens.
	The Universe expands.		All matter is compressed to a point.
1	The Big Bang happens.		Gravity starts to make the Universe contract.

Q4   The **visible** matter in the Universe gives about **4%** of the **gravity**
that would be needed to slow the **expansion** of the Universe right down to a **stop**.

a)   Imagine the **dark matter** in the Universe has **30 times** the mass of the visible matter.
How will the Universe end in this case?

....

b)   Imagine the dark matter has a **much smaller** mass than that of the visible matter.
What will happen in this case?

....

Q5   Tick the correct box to show whether each of these statements is **true** or **false**.

		true	false
a)	We do not know what any of the dark matter in the Universe is.	☐	☐
b)	We can measure approximately how fast the Universe is expanding.	☐	☐
c)	The Oscillating Universe Theory states that the Universe is in an endless cycle of contraction and expansion.	☐	☐
d)	There are no unsolved problems in astrophysics.	☐	☐

Mixed Questions — P1b Topics 11 & 12

Q1   EM radiation can be extremely **useful**.

a) Using the boxes below, number the following types of EM radiation in order of **decreasing** frequency (1 = highest frequency). Write down one use for each type of radiation.

☐   Ultraviolet   ....

☐   X-rays   ....

☐   Infrared   ....

b) Low intensity light can be used for **iris scanning**. Write down one advantage and one disadvantage of using iris scanning as a form of identification.

Advantage: ....

Disadvantage: ....

c) SETI is an Earth-based project that searches for **narrow band radio waves** from space.

i) What does SETI stand for? ....

ii) Why are they only interested in narrow band waves rather than all radio waves?

....

....

d) Explain how the **red-shift** of EM radiation can be used to show that the Universe is expanding.

....

....

e) What are the two possibilities for the eventual fate of the Universe?

....

Q2   The Sun is roughly halfway through its stable phase.

a) What will happen to the Sun at the end of this stable phase?

....

b) Will the Sun end up as a neutron star? Explain your answer.

....

c) Unlike the Sun, planets cannot produce their own light. Explain why they can sometimes be seen in the night sky.

....

Mixed Questions — P1b Topics 11 & 12

Q3   Earthquakes cause seismic waves to travel through the Earth.

a)   i)   Which type of seismic wave can travel through both solids and liquids? ....

ii)   Is it a transverse or longitudinal wave? ....

b)   Both types of wave curve as they travel through the Earth.

i)   Write down the name for this wave behaviour. Does the speed of the waves alter?

....

ii)   About halfway through the Earth, the path of the P-waves kinks. Explain why.

....

c)   Earthquakes are one of the possible consequences of a near-Earth object (NEO) striking Earth. Give one other possible consequence of an NEO collision with Earth.

....

Q4   A space probe is sent to **remotely** observe Mars.

a)   The probe has a mass of 3200 kg and is accelerating at 9.2 m/s². Calculate the force on the probe.

....

b)   Write down one disadvantage of using remote sensing rather than sending human explorers.

....

c)   The probe sends **analogue** radio signals at a frequency of 95.6 MHz back to Earth. (Use v = 3 × 10⁸ m/s.)

i)   Calculate the wavelength of the radio signals.

....

ii)   How long does it take the signals to reach Earth if the probe is 100 000 000 km away?

....

iii)   Describe the main difference between an analogue and digital signal.

....

....

d)   What lies between Mars and Jupiter? ....

e)   So far, there have been no manned missions to Mars. Write down one of the ill effects such a long space flight could have on astronauts and how this could be reduced.

....

f)   Why would an astronaut on Mars weigh less than on Earth even though his mass stayed the same?

....

Speed and Velocity

Q1 A pulse of **laser light** takes **1.3 seconds** to travel from the Moon to the Earth. The **speed of light** is approximately 3×10^8 **m/s**.

You'll need to rearrange the speed formula.

How far away is the Moon from the Earth? Give your answer in km.

....

Q2 Tom starts his journey to school by **walking** to the bus stop — this takes **10 minutes** at a speed of **1 m/s**. Next, Tom catches the **bus** and travels for **20 minutes** at an average speed of **15 m/s**. Tom usually has to **run** the last bit of the journey, which takes **5 minutes** at an average speed of **3 m/s**.

a) How many seconds does each part of Tom's journey take?

....

....

b) How far does Tom travel in total?

....

....

c) What is Tom's average speed for the whole journey? Assume there's no wait at the bus stop.

....

Q3 **Speed cameras** can be used to catch speeding motorists. The section of road in the diagram below has a **speed limit** of **50 miles per hour**.

a) 1 mile = 1609 metres. Show that 50 miles per hour is about the same speed as 22 m/s.

....

b) The diagram below shows a car passing in front of a speed camera. The two pictures show the position of the car 0.5 s apart. The distance between each white line on the road is 5 metres.

Was the car breaking the speed limit? Show your working.

....

Top Tips: Speed and velocity are both how fast you're going, and are calculated in the same way. The only difference between speed and velocity is that velocity has direction. Simple.

Speed and Velocity

Q4   Ealing is about **12 km** west of Marble Arch. It takes a
tube train **20 minutes** to get to Marble Arch from Ealing.

Only **one** of the following statements is true. Circle the appropriate letter.

    A   The average speed of the train is 60 m/s.

    B   The average velocity of the train is 10 m/s.

    C   The average velocity of the train is 60 m/s due east.

    D   The average speed of the train is 10 m/s.

    E   The average velocity of the train is 10 m/s due west.

Q5   A **hare** challenges a **tortoise** to a **race**. The hare is so confident he'll win that he
takes a nap on the way — he sleeps too long and the tortoise ends up winning.
Here are some facts and figures about the race:

The **tortoise** ran at a constant speed of **5 m/s** throughout the race — pretty impressive.

The **hare** ran at **10 m/s** for **300 s** before falling asleep. He slept for **600 s** and then carried on at
10 m/s towards the finish line.

The length of the **race track** was **5000 m**.

a)   How far did the hare travel before falling asleep?

....

b)   Add the information about the hare's run to the graph below.

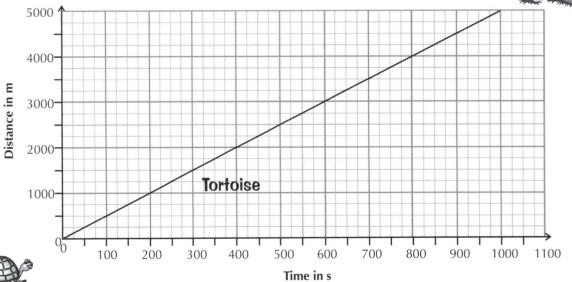

c)   When did the tortoise overtake the hare?

....

d)   How long did the tortoise have to wait at the finish line before the hare arrived?

....

Acceleration and Velocity-Time Graphs

Q1   An egg is dropped from the top of the Eiffel tower.
It hits the ground after **8 seconds**, at a speed of **80 m/s**.

   a)   Calculate the egg's acceleration. ....

   b)   How long did it take for the egg to reach a velocity of 40 m/s?

   ....

Q2   Below is a **velocity-time graph** for the descent of a **lunar lander**.
It accelerates due to the pull of gravity from the Moon.

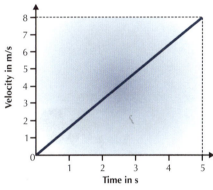

Use the graph to calculate
the lander's acceleration.

....

....

....

Q3   A car accelerates at **2 m/s²**. After **4 seconds** it reaches a speed of **24 m/s**.

   How fast was it going before it started to accelerate?

   ....

   ....

Q4   Describe the **type of motion** happening at each of the labelled points on the velocity-time graph.

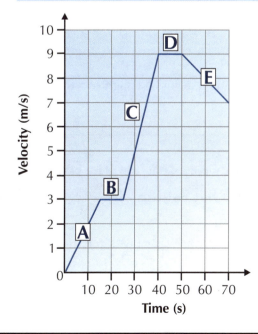

(A) ....

(B) ....

(C) ....

(D) ....

(E) ....

Forces

Q1 A bear rides a bike north at a constant speed.

a) Label the forces acting on the bear.

....

....

b) The bear brakes and slows down.
Are the forces balanced **as** he slows
down? If not, which direction is the
overall force in?

....

....

Q2 A teapot sits on a table.

a) Explain why it **doesn't** sink into the table.

....

b) Jane picks up the teapot and hangs it from the ceiling by a rope.
What vertical forces now act on the teapot?

....

c) The rope breaks and the teapot accelerates towards the floor.

i) Are the vertical forces balanced?

....

ii) The teapot hits the floor without breaking and bounces upwards.
Which force causes the teapot to bounce upwards?

....

Q3 Samantha tests the **grip** of her favourite car tyre by dragging it across a **rough surface**.

Choose the correct options to complete her conclusions.

- When I first pulled it, the tyre didn't move.
  This showed that the forces acting on the tyre were *in balance* / *unbalanced*.

- When the tyre just started to move, the force I was pulling with was
  greater than / *equal to* the frictional force.

- While the tyre was moving with a steady speed, the force I was pulling with
  was *greater than* / *equal to* the frictional force.

Friction Forces and Terminal Velocity

Q1   Use the words below to complete the paragraph about a **skydiver**.

accelerates   decelerates   less   greater   decrease   balances   increase   constant

When a skydiver jumps out of a plane, his weight is .... than his air

resistance, so he .... downwards. This causes his air resistance to

.... until it .... his weight. At this point, his

velocity is .... When his parachute opens, his air resistance is

.... than his weight, so he .... This causes his air

resistance to .... until it .... his weight. Then his

velocity is .... once again.

Q2   Which of the following will **reduce** the drag force on an aeroplane?
Tick any appropriate boxes.

☐ flying higher (where the air is thinner)   ☐ carrying less cargo

☐ flying more slowly   ☐ making the plane more streamlined

Q3   A scientist plans to investigate **gravity** by dropping a hammer and a feather from a tall building.
Two onlookers predict what will happen. Say whether each is right or wrong, and explain why.

Paola: "They will land at the same time — gravity is the same for both."

Guiseppe: "The feather will reach its terminal velocity before the hammer."

a)   Paola is **right** / **wrong** because ....

....

b)   Guiseppe is **right** / **wrong** because ....

....

Q4   Mavis is investigating **drag** by dropping balls into a measuring cylinder
full of oil and timing how long they take to reach the bottom.
She does the experiment with a **golf ball**, a **glass marble** and a **ball bearing**.

From this experiment, can Mavis draw any conclusions about
the effect of size on drag? Explain your answer.

....

....

Friction Forces and Terminal Velocity

Q5   The graph shows how the **velocity** of a **skydiver** changes before and after he opens his parachute.

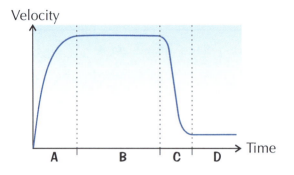

For each of the four regions A-D say whether the force of **weight** or **air resistance** is greater, or if they are **equal**.

	weight is greater	air resistance is greater	both equal
Region A:	☐	☐	☐
Region B:	☐	☐	☐
Region C:	☐	☐	☐
Region D:	☐	☐	☐

Q6   Two skydivers jump out of a plane. Kate opens her parachute after **3 seconds**, when she is still accelerating rapidly. Alison doesn't open her parachute yet but uses her video camera to film Kate's skydive. On the film Kate's parachute appears to pull her suddenly **upwards** when it opens.

a)   Is Kate really moving upwards? Explain your answer. ....

....

b)   Describe how Kate's velocity changes when her parachute opens. ....

....

Q7   On **Venus**, atmospheric pressure is about **90 times** that on Earth, but the gravitational field strength is about the same.
On **Mars**, atmospheric pressure is about **1/100th** of that on Earth and the gravitational field strength is less than half that on Earth.

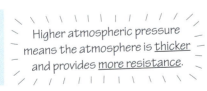

Higher atmospheric pressure means the atmosphere is _thicker_ and provides _more resistance_.

Probes which land on other planets often need parachutes to slow them down during their descent. What **size** of parachute would you recommend, relative to a parachute used on Earth, for:

a)   landing on Venus: ....

b)   landing on Mars: ....

Top Tips: When objects move through the air at high speed, the air resistance is proportional to the object's **velocity squared**. That's why, for skydivers, air resistance soon balances their weight and they reach terminal velocity. It's also why **driving** very fast is very **inefficient**.

Forces and Acceleration

Q1 Sue is driving the school bus at a **steady speed** along a straight level road.
Tick the boxes next to any of the following statements that are true.

☐ The driving force of the engine is bigger than the friction and air resistance combined.

☐ There are no forces acting on the bus.

☐ The driving force of the engine is equal to the friction and air resistance combined.

☐ No force is required to keep the bus moving.

Q2 State whether the forces acting on the following items are **balanced** or **unbalanced**, and explain your reasoning.

a) A **cricket ball** slowing down as it rolls along the outfield.

....

b) A **car** going round a roundabout at a steady 30 mph.

....

c) A **vase** knocked off a window ledge.

....

d) A **satellite** orbiting over a fixed point on the Earth's surface.

....

e) A **bag of rubbish** ejected from a spacecraft in empty space.

....

Q3 The table below shows the **masses** and **maximum accelerations** of four different antique cars.

Car	Mass (kg)	Maximum acceleration (m/s²)
Disraeli 9000	800	5
Palmerston 6i	1560	0.7
Heath TT	950	3
Asquith 380	790	2

Write down the names of the four cars in order of increasing driving force.

1. ....   2. ....

3. ....   4. ....

Forces and Acceleration

Q4 The diagram below shows the **forces** acting on an aeroplane.

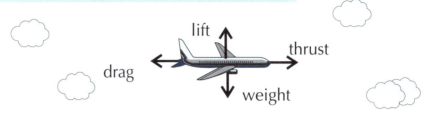

lift

thrust

drag

weight

a) The aircraft is flying horizontally at a constant speed of 200 m/s. Which of the following statements about the aeroplane is true? Circle the appropriate letter.

    A   The thrust is bigger than the drag and the lift is bigger than the weight.

    B   The thrust is smaller than the drag and the lift is equal to the weight.

    C   The thrust is equal to the drag and the lift is bigger than the weight.

    D   The thrust is equal to the drag and the lift is equal to the weight.

b) What happens to the forces as the plane descends for landing and slows down to 100 m/s? Choose the correct options to complete the following statements:

    i)   The thrust is **greater than** / **less than** / **equal to** the drag.

    ii) The lift is **greater than** / **less than** / **equal to** the weight.

Remember — the plane is losing height as well as slowing down.

Q5 Use the words supplied to fill in the blanks.

proportional	force	reaction	stationary	accelerates	opposite
constant	resultant	inversely	balanced		

If the forces on an object are .... , it's either .... or

moving at a .... speed.

If an object has a .... force acting on it, it .... in the

direction of the .... The acceleration is .... to the

force and .... to the mass.

For every action there is an equal and ....

Q6 A car tows a caravan along a road. At a **constant speed**, the pulling force of the car and the opposing reaction **force** of the caravan are **equal**. Which statement correctly describes the forces between the caravan and the car when the **car accelerates**? Tick the appropriate box.

☐ "The caravan's reaction force cancels out the pulling force of the car, so the caravan won't accelerate."

☐ "The caravan's reaction force is at a right angle to the force pulling the car, so the two forces don't affect one another."

☐ "The car's pulling force accelerates the caravan. The caravan's reaction force acts on the car, not the caravan."

Forces and Acceleration

Q7 Which picture shows the **weight (w)** and **reaction force (R)** of a car on a slope?
Tick the appropriate box.

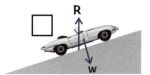 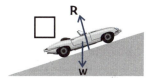 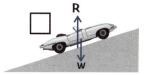 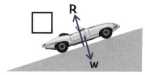

Q8 A very heavily laden **camper van** with a mass of **2500 kg** has a driving force of **2900 N** and needs a force of **1500 N** to climb a hill at constant speed. Would it be able to **overtake** a tractor which is accelerating at **0.6 m/s²**? (Assume both vehicles are travelling at the same speed to begin with.)

....

....

Q9 Bill is hammering a nail into the wall.
The hammer hits the nail at a speed of **5 m/s** and takes **0.01 s** to stop.

a) What is the hammer's deceleration?

....

b) The mass of the hammer is 0.5 kg. Calculate the **force** the nail exerts on the hammer.

....

c) Complete the following force diagram.

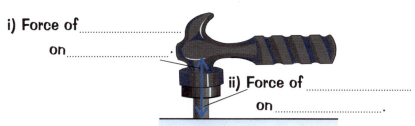

i) Force of............................
        on............................

ii) Force of ....
        on ....

Ben decides to have a go at hammering in the nail. He can only get the hammer up to a speed of 2.5 m/s rather than 5 m/s. The hammer also stops in 0.01 s.

d) Explain why Ben's hammering will exert a smaller force on the nail than Bill's.

....

....

Top Tips: Make sure that you learn the formula **F = m × a**. It really will be worth your while, as without it you won't be able to calculate mass, acceleration or force in the exam.

Stopping Distances

Q1 Stopping distance and braking distance are not the same thing.

   a) What is meant by 'braking distance'?

     ....

   b) Use the words in the box to complete the following word equations.

braking	speed	reaction time	thinking

     i) Thinking distance = ... × ....

     ii) Stopping distance = ... distance + ... distance.

Q2 Will the following factors affect **thinking** distance, **braking** distance or **both**? Write them in the relevant columns of the table.

tiredness   road surface   weather   speed   diesel spills

    alcohol   tyre tread   brakes   load   ice

Thinking Distance	Braking Distance

Q3 A car joins a motorway and changes speed from 30 mph to 60 mph. Which one of the following statements is **true**? Tick the appropriate box.

☐ Thinking distance will double and braking distance will more than double.

☐ Thinking distance will stay the same but braking distance will double.

☐ The total stopping distance will decrease.

Q4 A car has just been driven through a **deep puddle**, making the brakes wet. Explain why this will **increase** the **stopping distance** of the car.

....

....

Car Safety

Q1 Circle the correct words or phrases to make the following statements **true**.

a) If the velocity of a moving object doubles, its **driving force** / **momentum** will double.

b) If you drop a suitcase out of a moving car, the car's momentum will **decrease** / **increase**.

c) When two objects collide the total momentum **changes** / **stays the same**.

d) When a force acts on an object its momentum **changes** / **stays the same**.

Q2 Calculate the **momentum** of a truck with a mass of 4500 kg that's travelling at 10 m/s.

....

Q3 A **750 kg car** is travelling at **30 m/s** along the motorway. It crashes into the barrier of the central reservation and is stopped in a period of **1.2 seconds**.

a) Find the size of the **average force** acting on the car as it stops.

....

....

b) Explain why the occupants of the car are likely to be less severely injured if they are wearing seatbelts made of slightly **stretchy** material.

....

....

Q4 The graph below shows the number of casualties from motorway traffic accidents in the country of Thornland.

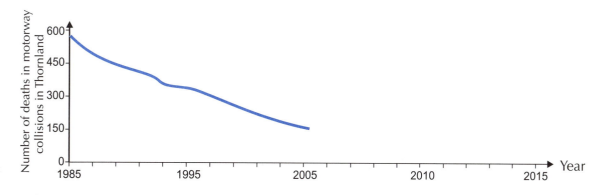

a) If the current trend continued, mark on the graph the point at which you would expect there to be **zero** casualties.

b) Explain why the trend is unlikely to continue in this way.

....

Taking Risks

Q1 The risk of my bus being late is **1 in 4**. Express this risk:

a) As a **fraction** ....

b) As a **decimal** .... c) As a **percentage** ....

Q2 Skydivers have a **reserve parachute** in case the main one fails.

a) Skydiving is a risky activity. Why do some people think it is worth the risk?

....

b) Suggest why having main **and** reserve parachutes reduces the risk of an accident.

....

Q3 Mr Burns is planning to build a new **power station**. The table shows the **risk** of four different types of power station **exploding** within 50 years.

Power Station	Risk of Explosion within 50 years
Coal	0.01
Oil	6/500
Nuclear	1.5%
Gas	0.014

An explosion would be a disaster — and cost Mr Burns loads of money. Which type of power station would you advise him to choose?

....

....

Q4 Some statistics have shown that **travelling by car** may be riskier than **travelling by plane**. Give two reasons why some people are happy to drive, but very scared of flying.

....

....

Q5 Susie and James are playing a board game using a six-sided dice. If they **roll a one**, they must miss the next turn.

a) Susie says the best way to work out the risk of rolling a one is just to use **probability**. Using her advice, what is the risk of rolling a one? Give your answer as a fraction.

....

b) James thinks the risk calculation should be based on **previous rolls** of the dice. James has rolled a one on two out of his last four turns. Use James' method to calculate the risk of rolling a one.

....

c) Whose method of risk assessment will give the most **accurate** answer? Give a reason for your answer.

....

Work and Kinetic Energy

Q1 Circle the correct words to make the following sentences true.

a) Work involves the transfer of **force** / **heat** / **energy**.

b) To do work **a force** / **an acceleration** must act over a **distance** / **time**.

c) Work is measured in **watts** / **joules**.

Q2 Indicate whether the following statements are **true** or **false**.

	True	False
a) Work is done when a toy car is pushed along the ground.	☐	☐
b) No work is done if a force is applied to an object which does not move.	☐	☐
c) Gravity does work on an apple that is not moving.	☐	☐
d) Gravity does work on an apple that falls out of a tree.	☐	☐

Q3 An elephant exerts a constant force of **1200 N** to push a donkey along a track at a steady **1 m/s**.

a) Calculate the work done by the elephant if the donkey moves **8 m**.

....

b) From where does the elephant get the energy to do this work? ....

c) Into what form(s) is this energy transferred when work is done on the donkey?

....

Q4 Ben's mass is 60 kg. He climbs a ladder. The rungs of the ladder are 20 cm apart.

a) What force(s) is Ben doing work **against** as he climbs?

....

b) As he climbs, what happens to the **energy** supplied by Ben's muscles?

....

....

20 cm

c) How much work does Ben do when he climbs **10 rungs**? (Ignore any 'wasted' energy.)
Assume that g = 10 N/kg.

....

....

d) How many rungs of the ladder must Ben climb before he has done **15 kJ** of work?
(Ignore any 'wasted' energy.) Assume that g = 10 N/kg.

....

....

Work and Kinetic Energy

Q5 Two tug-of-war teams compete to win a bunch of grapes. There are three men and two women in each team.

At the start of the contest, everyone pulls as hard as they can — the women can exert a force of 150 N each and the men can exert a force of 200 N each.

a) When everyone pulls with their maximum force, what is the work done by each team?

....

b) After a while, one of the men stumbles and falls over. Everyone else keeps pulling as hard as they can, but the other side manage to drag their opponents over the winning line — a distance of five metres. How much **work** have they done in order to win the grapes?

....

....

Q6 Find the **kinetic energy** of a 200 kg tiger running at a speed of 9 m/s.

....

....

Q7 A golf ball is hit and given 9 J of kinetic energy. The ball's velocity is 20 m/s. What is its **mass**?

....

....

....

Q8 A 60 kg skydiver jumps out of an aeroplane and free-falls. Find the skydiver's **speed** if she has 90 750 J of kinetic energy.

....

....

....

> ## Top Tips:
> Work is done when a force makes things **move**. E.g. an Arctic explorer pulling a sledge over the ice exerts a **force** on the sledge which makes it **move** a certain **distance**. To get the sledge moving (from stationary), chemical energy from the explorer's food is transferred into kinetic energy (of the moving sledge) and into heat (because of friction between the sledge and the ice and in making the explorer a bit hot). Once the sledge is moving at a steady speed, energy is still being transferred — enough to keep on overcoming friction (and to keep our brave hero all hot and sweaty).

Electrical and Potential Energy

Q1   Dale loves a bit of DIY, and is drilling holes to put up some shelves.
His electric drill is attached to a **12 V** battery and uses a current of **2.3 A**.

a)   Write down the equation that relates current, voltage, electrical energy and time.

    ....

b)   If it takes Dale 30 seconds to drill one hole, how much energy
will be transformed by the motor if he drills **eight** holes?

    ....

    ....

Q2   Jerry was rescued from the sea by helicopter. He was lifted **10 m** using an electric motor.

a)   Jerry weighs 70 kg. Calculate the **potential energy** he gained. (g = 10 N/kg)

    ....

b)   The electric motor uses a voltage of 40 V and a current of 5 A.
Calculate how long the motor would take to transform the amount of energy that Jerry gained?

    ....

c)   The motor would actually take much longer than this to lift Jerry. Explain why.

    ....

Q3   Fred works at a DIY shop. He has to load **28** flagstones onto the delivery truck.
Each flagstone has a mass of **25 kg** and has to be lifted **1.2 m** onto the truck.

a)   How much gravitational potential energy does one flagstone
gain when lifted onto the truck? (g = 10 N/kg)

    ....

b)   What is the **total gravitational potential energy** gained by the flagstones after they are all loaded
onto the truck?

    ....

c)   How much **work** does Fred do loading the truck?

    ....

    ....

Conservation of Energy

Q1 The light bulb in this **torch** is powered by a battery.

a) What energy transformation is taking place in the battery?

.... energy to .... energy.

b) What energy transformations are taking place in the light bulb?

.... energy to .... energy and .... energy.

Q2 Mr Coles is about to demonstrate the **conservation of energy**.
He holds a heavy pendulum up by a window and lets go.

a) Explain why he can be sure that the pendulum won't smash the window when it swings back.

....

b) When the pendulum actually does swing back, it doesn't quite reach the height of the window again. Where has the potential energy gone?

....

Q3 Dave the frog **jumps** off the ground at a speed of 10 m/s.

a) If Dave has a mass of 500 g, what is his kinetic energy as he leaves the ground?

....

b) What is Dave's maximum possible potential energy?

....

c) What is the maximum height Dave can reach?

....

d) In practice, why won't Dave reach this height? (Explain your answer in terms of energy.)

....

Q4 Kim dives off a **5 m** high diving board and belly-flops into the swimming pool below.

a) If Kim's mass is 100 kg, calculate her kinetic energy as she hits the water.

....

b) At what speed will Kim be falling as she hits the water?

....

Power

Q1   Complete this passage by using the words provided.

heat	energy	100	rate	light	watts	joules

Power is the .... of doing work, or how much .... is

transferred per second. It is measured in .... or .... per

second.

A 100 W light bulb transfers .... joules of electrical energy into

.... and .... each second.

Q2   Catherine and Sally decide to run up a set of stairs to see who can get to the top more quickly. Catherine has a mass of **46 kg** and Sally has a mass of **48 kg**.

g = 10 N/kg

a)   The top of the stairs is **5 m** above ground.
Calculate the gain in **potential energy** for:

i)   Catherine ....

ii) Sally ....

b)   Catherine won the race in **6.2 s**, while Sally took **6.4 s**.
Which girl generated more **power**?

....

....

Q3   Tom likes to build model boats. His favourite boat is the Carter, which has a motor power of **150 W**.

a)   How much **energy** does the Carter transfer in **10 minutes**?

....

b)   The petrol for the boat's motor can supply **30 kJ/ml**.
What volume of petrol is used up in **10 minutes**?

....

c)   Tom decides to get a model speed boat which transfers **120 kJ** in 10 minutes.
What is the **power** of the engine?

....

Top Tips: Power is a measure of the energy transferred, or work done, within a certain time — the faster a person or machine can get a task done, the more powerful it is. Just think, if you were a power-mad ruler you could try take over the world in the blink of an eye, mwah haa ha ha ha...

Circular Motion

Q1 Which of the following is the **best definition** of acceleration? Circle the appropriate letter.

A an increase in speed **B** an increase in velocity **C** a change in speed
D a change in direction **E** a change in velocity

Q2 A **satellite** orbiting the Earth travels at a constant speed.

a) Is the satellite **accelerating**? Explain your answer.

....

b) Put a tick next to each **true** statement below.

☐ If a body is accelerating then there must be a resultant force acting on it.

☐ The forces acting on a body going round in a circle at a steady speed must be balanced.

☐ If there is no resultant force acting on a body then it carries on moving in a straight line at the same speed.

c) What is the general name for a force that keeps a body moving in a circular path?

....

d) Draw lines to match up the following bodies with the force that keeps them moving in a circle.

A runner running round a circular track	Gravity
A satellite in orbit round the Earth	Tension
The seats at the ends of the spokes of a spinning fairground ride	Friction

Q3 Circle the **correct** options in these sentences.

a) The greater the mass of a body, the smaller / **greater** the force needed to keep it moving in a circle.

b) It takes a greater force to keep a body moving in a **smaller** / larger circle.

c) A cyclist rides round a circular track at a speed of 20 m/s.
The frictional force between his tyres and the track is 1467 N.
He speeds up to 21 m/s — the frictional force changes to **1617 N** / **1331 N**.

Q4 The diagram below shows a clock with hands that move **steadily** around the clock-face.

a) Draw and label with 'A' an arrow on the diagram to show the direction of the **velocity** of the tip of the **minute hand**.

b) Draw and label with 'B' an arrow to show the direction of the **acceleration** of the tip of the **hour hand**.

Circular Motion

Q5 The diagram below shows a car going round a roundabout.
The car is travelling at a **constant speed** of 10 m/s.

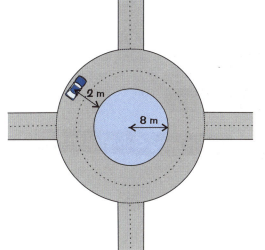

a) Is the car **accelerating**? How do you know this?

....

....

b) Draw an **arrow** on the diagram to show the direction
of the **force** acting on the car.

c) The mass of the car is **1000 kg**. Calculate the size of
the force acting on the car.

....

....

d) A **large truck** joins the roundabout. Would you expect the **centripetal force** acting on the truck to
be **larger** or **smaller** than the force acting on the car? Give a reason for your answer.

....

e) It starts to **rain**. Why will the drivers not be able to drive as fast on the roundabout?

....

....

Q6 The Earth orbits the Sun because there is a **centripetal force** on it due to the Sun's gravity.
The size of this force is **3.6×10^{22} N**.

The radius of Earth's orbit around the Sun is 1.5×10^{11} m and the mass of the Earth is 6.0×10^{24} kg.

a) Using the data above calculate the **speed** at which the Earth orbits the Sun.

....

b) The diagram shows the Moon orbiting the
Earth due to the Earth's gravity. Use the information
on the diagram to calculate the **mass** of the Moon.

....

....

....

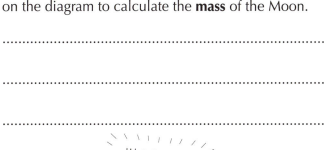

Watch out for
changes of units.

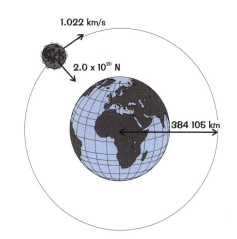

1.022 km/s

2.0×10^{20} N

384 105 km

Roller Coasters

Q1 A roller coaster and passengers are stationary at the top of a ride. At this point they have a gravitational potential energy of **300 kJ**. Each full carriage has a mass of 750 kg.

a) Draw lines to connect the correct energy statement with each stage of the roller coaster.

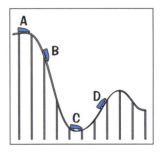

A

B

C

D

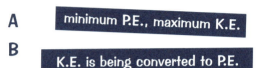

A minimum P.E., maximum K.E.

B K.E. is being converted to P.E.

maximum P.E.

P.E. is being converted to K.E.

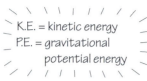

K.E. = kinetic energy
P.E. = gravitational
        potential energy

b) **i)** When the roller coaster is at half its original height, how much **kinetic energy** should it have?

....

ii) Calculate the speed of each roller coaster carriage at this point.

....

iii) Explain why in real life the speed is **less** than this.

....

Q2 You have been asked to **design** a new roller coaster for a theme park.

a) Write down two **safety features** that you could include in your design.

....

b) Write down two benefits that your new ride could have for the **local community**.

....

Q3 On the 'Cliff Edge' roller coaster, the **1200 kg** carriages are **stopped** at the top of a huge vertical drop before being released. The roller coaster reaches a speed of **22 m/s** at the bottom of the drop before going into several loop-the-loops.

a) Calculate the height of the vertical drop.

....

....

b) What two forces act on you during the loop-the-loop? ....

c) Explain why you feel a lot lighter at the top of the loop than at the bottom.

....

Einstein's Relativity

Q1   Isaac and Albert are measuring the **speed of the light** produced from the headlights of a spaceship.

Isaac measures the speed of the light when the spaceship is **still**. He finds that the light is travelling towards him at **300 million m/s**.

Albert also measures the speed of the light, but this time the spaceship is **moving** towards him at a speed of **100 million m/s**.

If Albert measures everything correctly, then what **speed** does he measure?

....

Q2   The **theory of relativity** was developed in several stages. Rearrange the stages below in the correct order by numbering the boxes 1 to 7.

☐   Einstein began his famous thought experiments about light, time and space.

☐   Newton developed his laws of motion.

☐   The theory made very precise new predictions (e.g. about the effects of motion on time).

☐   Developments in technology enabled these predictions to be tested.

☐   Discovery that the speed of light is always the same can't be explained using Newton's laws.

☐   General acceptance of the theory of relativity.

☐   Einstein produced his theory of relativity.

Q3   The theory of relativity only predicted different results from **Newton's laws of motion** for objects moving at incredibly fast speeds or in incredibly strong gravitational fields.

a)   Newton's laws were developed in the 17th century. Why did it take around **200 hundred years** before scientists realised that they were slightly wrong?

....

b)   At everyday speeds and gravity, Einstein's theory predicts exactly the same results as Newton's. Explain why this is an important feature of Einstein's relativity and adds weight to the evidence that his theory is valid.

....

c)   In some situations the two theories predicted different outcomes. Outline how this was tested using **atomic clocks**.

....

....

72

Einstein's Relativity

Q4   Many theories, like relativity, are based on **thought experiments**.

a)   What is meant by a "thought experiment"?

....

b)   Why are thought experiments extremely useful when creating new theories?

....

c)   Apart from experimental evidence, name a factor that would increase the chances of a theory being accepted.

Hint — Einstein was not the only scientist looking at the speed of light.

....

Q5   **Cosmic rays** can produce particles called muons.

a)   What happens to the lifetime of muons when they move close to the speed of light?

....

b)   Does this support or go against the prediction made by relativity? Explain your answer.

....

....

Q6   Some things predicted by relativity have not yet been observed.

a)   Explain why this doesn't prove that the theory of relativity is wrong.

....

b)   Scientific theories can never be proved right — they can only be proved wrong. Why is this?

....

....

c)   Why does the development of new **measuring instruments** sometimes lead to support for or against a scientific idea?

....

Top Tips: Many scientists like to think they know an awful lot about their subject, so if someone comes along with a radical new idea, it's often hard for them to accept it. Testing the new idea is a good way of helping people to believe it — if it predicts the right answer of course.
P.S. If you spot a gravity wave then tell everyone about it — just make sure you get a photo first.

Mixed Questions — P2 Topics 9 & 10

Q1 Norman loves trainspotting. As a special treat, he not only notes
the train numbers but plots a **distance-time** graph for two of the trains.

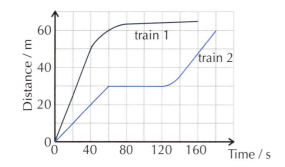

a) For how long is train 2 stationary?

....

b) Both trains start at a steady speed.
How can you tell this from the graph?

....

c) Calculate the initial speed of the faster train.

....

d) Describe the motion of train 1 between 40 s and 80 s.

....

Q2 In the film 'Crouching Sparrow, Hidden Beaver', a **95 kg** dummy is
dropped **60 m** from the top of a building. (Assume that g = 10 m/s².)

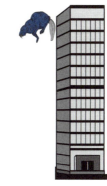

a) Sketch a distance-time graph and a velocity-time graph for the dummy
from the moment it is dropped until just after it hits the ground.
(Ignore air resistance and assume the dummy does not reach a terminal speed.)

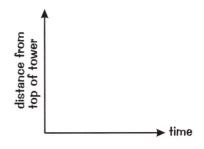

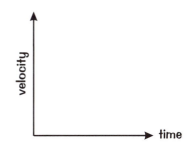

b) Do any forces act on the dummy when it lies still on the ground (after falling)? If so, what are they?

....

c) The take doesn't go to plan so the dummy is lifted back to the top of the building using a motor.

i) How much work is done on the dummy to get it to the top of the building?

....

ii) The useful power output of the motor is **760 W**.
How long does it take to get the dummy to the top of the building?

....

iii) If the motor uses the mains (**230 V**), calculate the current. (Assume it is 100% efficient.)

....

Mixed Questions — P2 Topics 9 & 10

Q3 Liz goes on a roller coaster. With her in it, the roller coaster carriage has a total mass of **1200 kg**.

a) What is the weight of the carriage? (Assume $g = 10$ m/s^2.)

....

b) At the start of the ride the carriage rises up to its highest point of **60 m** above the ground and stops. Calculate its gain in potential energy.

....

c) Write down the principle of the conservation of energy.

....

....

d) The carriage then falls to a third of its maximum height. Assuming there is no air resistance or friction, calculate the speed of the carriage at this point.

....

....

....

e) Along the way, the carriage does a loop-the-loop. Explain why Liz feels much heavier at the bottom of the loop than at the top.

....

....

f) At the end of the ride, the carriage slows down, decelerating at **6.4 m/s^2**. How long does it take the carriage to slow down from **18 m/s** and come to a stop?

....

....

g) **i)** Write down one safety feature that should be installed on a roller coaster.

....

  ii) Suggest two ways a new theme park would affect the surrounding community.

....

....

Mixed Questions — P2 Topics 9 & 10

Q4 A sky-diver jumps out of an aeroplane.
His weight is **700 N**.

a) What force causes him to accelerate downwards?

....

b) After **10 s** he is falling at a steady speed of **60 m/s**.
State the force of air resistance that is acting on him.

....

c) He now opens his parachute, which increases the air resistance to **2000 N**.
Explain what happens immediately after he opens the parachute.

....

....

d) After falling with his parachute open for **5 s**, the sky-diver is travelling at a steady speed of **4 m/s**.
What is the air resistance force now?

....

Q5 Dexter is scared of flying. He decides to take a risk and face his fear by travelling on a high speed aeroplane with his favourite atomic clock.

a) Write down two factors which influence a person's willingness to take risks.

1. ....

2. ....

b) Trying not to think about flying, Dexter calculates the chance of getting a tasty aeroplane meal as **1/320** and decides not to risk it. Convert this fraction into a percentage.

....

c) i) How would the time on Dexter's clock be different from that on a stationary atomic clock?

....

ii) What theory does this observation support?

....

iii) Give one reason why it took so long for this theory to be accepted.

....

Mixed Questions — P2 Topics 9 & 10

Q6   Cherie and Tony rob a bank. They escape in a getaway car with a mass of **2100 kg** and travel at a constant speed of **90 km/h** along a straight, level road.

a)   Is there a resultant force on the car? Explain your answer.

....

b)   Calculate the momentum of the car.

....

c)   A police car swings into the middle of the road and stops ahead of Cherie's car. Cherie brakes with a reaction time of **0.7 s** and the car comes to a halt **3.0 s** after she hits the brakes.

   i)   Calculate her thinking distance.

   ....

   ii)   Write down one factor that could affect Cherie's thinking distance.

   ....

   iii)   Assuming the car decelerates uniformly, find the force acting on the braking car.

   ....

   ....

d)   Explain how seat belts would have helped keep Cherie and Tony safer if they had crashed.

....

Q7   The V-T graph below shows part of a car's journey round a racing track.

a)   Describe the motion of the car between:

   i)   40 s and 70 s ....

   ii)   100 s and 130 s ....

b)   Calculate how many metres the car travelled at 160 km/h.

   ....

   ....

Velocity / km/h vs Time / s

c)   The car whizzes around a semicircular bend on the track with a radius of 180 m.
The car has a mass of 560 kg and is going at 38 m/s. Calculate the centripetal force on the car.

....

....

Ionising Radiation

Q1 Complete the passage using the words given below. You will not have to use all the words.

> ions   less   more   electrons   further   less far   protons

When ionising radiation hits atoms, it sometimes knocks ....

off the atoms and makes them into .... Radiations that are

more ionising travel .... into a material and tend to cause

.... damage in the material they have penetrated.

Q2 Complete the table below by choosing the correct word from each column.

Radiation Type	Ionising power weak/moderate/ strong	Charge positive/none/ negative	Relative mass no mass/ small/large	Penetrating power low/moderate/ high	Relative speed slow/fast/ very fast
alpha					
beta					
gamma					

Q3 a) For each sentence, tick the correct box to show whether it is **true** or **false**.

True False

i) All nuclear radiation is positively charged. ☐ ☐

ii) Gamma radiation has no mass because it is an EM wave. ☐ ☐

iii) Alpha is the slowest and most strongly ionising type of radiation. ☐ ☐

iv) Beta particles are electrons, so they do not come from the nucleus. ☐ ☐

b) For each of the false sentences, write out a correct version.

....

....

....

When Terry went to school they didn't teach him to avoid Iionising radiation.

Ionising Radiation

Q4 Radiation from three sources — A, B and C — was directed towards target sheets of **paper**, **aluminium** and **lead**. Counters were used to detect where radiation passed through the target sheets.

Source A — the radiation was partially absorbed by the lead.
Source B — the radiation was stopped by the paper.
Source C — the radiation was stopped by the aluminium.

What type of radiation is emitted by:

source A? ...., source B? ...., source C? ....

Q5 Explain clearly why gamma rays are **less ionising** than alpha particles.

....

....

....

Q6 Write down the atomic number and mass number for each type of radiation.

a) **alpha**   atomic number = ...   mass number = ...

b) **beta**   atomic number = ...   mass number = ...

c) **gamma**   atomic number = ...   mass number = ...

Q7 X-rays and gamma rays are electromagnetic waves.

a) Describe how gamma rays are released.

....

b) How are X-rays produced?

....

Top Tips: Alpha, beta and gamma radiation all have different properties, but there's a nice predictable relationship between those properties. So make sure you know, for example, the relationship between relative mass and penetrating ability — one increases while the other decreases. It's the same kind of thing for relative mass and speed.

Background Radiation

Q1   Which of the following are **true**? Circle the appropriate letters.

A   About half of the UK's background radiation comes from radon gas.

B   The nuclear industry is responsible for about 10% of background radiation in the UK.

C   If there were no radioactive substances on Earth, there would be no background radiation.

Q2   The level of background radiation varies from place to place. For each of the following, indicate whether the background level will be **higher** or **lower** than average and explain your answer.

a)   In an aeroplane at high altitude, the level will be **higher** / **lower** than average because:

....

b)   In a mine, the level will usually be **higher** / **lower** than average because:

....

c)   In houses built above granite rocks, the level will usually be **higher** / **lower** than average because:

....

Q3   Peter did an experiment to compare equal quantities of two radioactive materials. Here are his results and conclusion:

Material tested	Radiation measured (counts per second)
None	50
Material A	200
Material B	400

CONCLUSION
"Both materials are radioactive.
Material B is twice as radioactive
as Material A."

Is Peter's conclusion correct? Give a reason for your answer.

....

....

Q4   The concentration of **radon** gas found in people's homes varies across the UK.

a)   Why does the concentration vary across the country?

....

b)   Explain why high concentrations of radon are dangerous.

....

c)   How can people in high radon areas reduce the radon concentration in their homes?

....

Atomic Structure

Q1 Fill in the blanks using the words below. Each word should be used only once.

radiation isotope element protons neutrons nuclei radioactive
Isotopes are atoms which have the same number of .... but different numbers of .... Some isotopes are .... Their .... are unstable, so they break down and spit out .... When this happens the nucleus often changes into a new ....

Q2 Indicate whether these sentences are **true** or **false**.

True False

a) The nucleus of an atom takes up almost no space compared to the whole atom. ☐ ☐

b) Most of an atom's mass is in the electrons. ☐ ☐

c) Atoms of the same element with the same number of neutrons are called isotopes. ☐ ☐

d) Radioactive decay speeds up at higher temperatures. ☐ ☐

Q3 The diagram shows uranium-238 decaying into thorium by alpha and gamma emission.

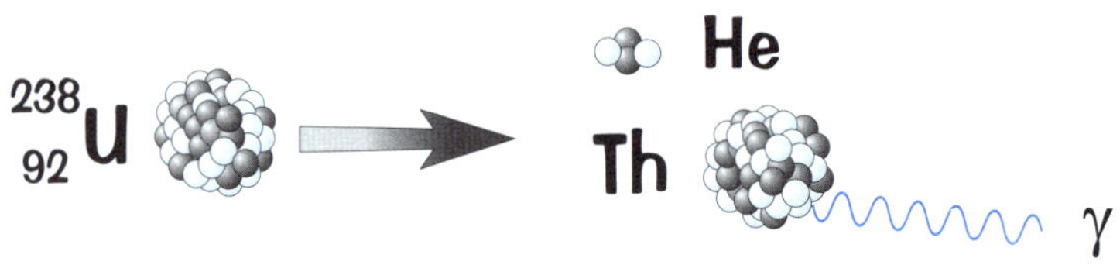

$$^{238}_{92}U \longrightarrow \text{He} \quad \text{Th} \quad \gamma$$

a) Does the **gamma ray** emission have an effect on the nucleus? If so, what is it?

....

b) Write the full nuclear equation for this decay, clearly showing the atomic and mass numbers.

....

Q4 Write the nuclear equations for the following decay processes.

a) An atom of thorium-234 ($^{234}_{90}$Th) emits a beta particle and a gamma ray and becomes an atom of protactinium.

....

b) An atom of radon-222 ($^{222}_{86}$Rn) emits an alpha particle and becomes an atom of polonium.

....

Half-Life

Q1   A radioactive isotope has a half-life of **60 years**.
Which of these statements describes this isotope correctly? Tick one box only.

In 60 years, half of the atoms in the material will have gone. ☐

In 30 years' time, only half the atoms will be radioactive. ☐

In 60 years' time, the count rate will be half what it is now. ☐

In about 180 years there will be almost no radioactivity left in the material. ☐

Q2   Sandra measures how the radioactivity of a sample changes with time.
The table shows some of her results.

Time (minutes)	0	10	20	30	40	80	160
Counts per minute	740	553	420	326	260	140	103

Count rate (cpm)

a) Use Sandra's results to draw a graph of counts per minute against time.

b) The counts per minute will never fall below 100. Suggest two reasons why.

....

....

c) Sandra calculates that the half-life of her sample is about 20 minutes. Explain how she worked this out. (You may find it useful to show some of the working on your graph.)

....

....

Time (mins)

Q3   The graph shows how the count rate of a radioactive isotope declines with time.

Count Rate (cpm)

Time (minutes)

a) What is the half-life of this isotope?

....

b) What was the count rate after 3 half-lives?

....

c) What fraction of the original radioactive nuclei will still be unstable after 5 half-lives?

....

d) After how long was the count rate down to 100? ....

Half-Life

Q4 The half-life of uranium-238 is **4500 million** years. The half-life of carbon-14 is **5730** years.

  a) What do the "238" in "uranium-238" and the "14" in "carbon-14" mean?

  ....

  ....

  b) If you start with a sample of each element and the two samples
have equal activity, which will lose its radioactivity most quickly?
Circle the correct answer.

  uranium-238   **carbon-14**

You'll need to change 6 minutes into seconds.

Q5 A radioactive isotope has a half-life of **40 seconds**.

  a) What fraction of the unstable nuclei will still be radioactive after 6 minutes?

  ....

  ....

  b) **i)** If the initial count rate of the sample was 8000 counts per minute,
what would be the approximate count rate after 6 minutes?

  ....

  ....

  ii) After how many whole **minutes** would the count rate have fallen below 10 counts per minute?

  ....

  ....

Q6 Peter was trying to explain half-life to his little brother. He said, "isotopes with
a long half-life are always more dangerous than those with a short half-life."

  Is Peter right? Explain your answer.

  ....

  ....

  ....

> **Top Tips:** Half-life tells you **how quickly** a source becomes **less radioactive**. If your source
> has a half-life of 50 years then after 100 years the count rate will be 1/4 of its original value. But if
> the half-life's 10 years, after 100 years the count rate will be less than 1/1000th of its original value.

Uses of Ionising Radiation

Q1　Complete the following paragraphs on radiotherapy using the words provided.

ill　centre　normal　kill　cells　focused　cancer　dose　radiotherapy

High doses of gamma radiation will .... living ....

Because of this, gamma radiation is used to treat .... This is called

....

Gamma rays are .... on the tumour using a wide beam. Damage to

.... cells can make the patient feel very .... This damage

is minimised by directing the radiation at the tumour and using the minimum

.... possible.

Q2　The table shows some commonly used radioisotopes and the type of radiation they emit.

a)　Which of these isotopes would be most
suitable for these applications?

i)　A smoke detector

....

ii)　To sterilise pre-packed food

....

Radioisotope	Decays by...
strontium-90	beta emission
americium-241	mainly alpha emission
cobalt-60	beta and gamma emission

b)　What further information about these isotopes would you want before you considered using them?

....

Q3　The following sentences explain how a smoke detector works, but they are in the wrong order.

Put them in order by labelling them 1 (first) to 6 (last).

☐　The circuit is broken so no current flows.

☐ 1　The radioactive source emits alpha particles.

☐　A current flows between the electrodes — the alarm stays off.

☐　The alarm sounds.

☐　The air between the electrodes is ionised by the alpha particles.

☐　A fire starts and smoke particles absorb the alpha radiation.

?

Uses of Ionising Radiation

Q4 The diagram shows how radiation can be used to sterilise surgical instruments.

a) What kind of radioactive source is used, and why? In your answer, mention the **type** of radiation emitted (α, β and γ) and the **half-life** of the source.

....

....

b) What is the purpose of the thick lead?

....

Q5 Iodine-131 is commonly used as a tracer in medicine.

a) Normal iodine has a mass number of 127. Why is it no good as a tracer?

....

b) The thyroid gland normally absorbs iodine.
Describe how iodine-131 can be used to detect if the thyroid gland is working properly.

....

....

....

Q6 A patient has a radioactive source injected into her body to test her kidneys.

A healthy kidney will get rid of the radioactive material quickly (to the bladder). Damaged kidneys take longer to do this.

The results of the test, for both the patient's kidneys, are shown opposite.

a) Explain how the doctor knew which kidney was working well and which was not.

....

....

b) Explain why an alpha source would **not** be suitable for this investigation.

....

....

P2 Topic 11 — Putting Radiation to Use

Radioactive Dating

Q1   Carbon-14 makes up about 1/10 000 000 of the carbon in the air.

a)   Name one gas in the air which contains carbon.

....

b)   What proportion of the carbon present in organisms alive now is carbon-14?

....

c)   What happens to the level of carbon-14 in a plant or animal after it dies?

....

Q2   A wooden spoon from an archaeological dig was found to have 1 part C-14 to 80 000 000 parts carbon. Work out when the wood was **living material**. (The half-life of C-14 is 5730 years.)

....

Q3   Uranium-238 has a half-life of 4.5 billion years.

a)   Explain how the decay of uranium can be used to date rocks.

....

Rock, 243 019 yrs, but young at heart. Cumbria based, GSOH. Likes: the outdoors. Dislikes: dogs, moss

Mal 45, seek curv foot mor

....

b)   A meteorite contains uranium-238 and lead-206 in a ratio of 1:3. How old is the meteorite?

....

Q4   A leather strap was found to have 1 part C-14 in 320 000 000 parts C-12.

a)   How many half-lives have occurred since the strap was a piece of skin on a living cow?

....

The half-life of C-14 is 5730 years

b)   How old would this make the strap?

....

c)   Explain how you could use a computer to reduce the error in measuring the strap's radioactivity.

....

....

Radioactive Dating

Q5 Professor Zuton is trying to discover the age of a Roman soldier's uniform discovered in boggy ground. He thinks it must be around 1800 years old. To find out if he's right, he uses carbon dating to test different parts of the uniform. Here are his results and notes.

Item	Age according to C-14 dating (years)	Notes
Leather belt	1800	
Woollen jacket	1200	This must be wrong. It should be older than that.
Wooden button	2100	This is older than I was expecting...

I don't really care how old it is, I just wanted some free clothes...

The professor is sure all the parts are about the same age. List four reasons why the test results might disagree.

1. ....

2. ....

3. ....

4. ....

Q6 a) Read the following conversation and decide if everyone is right or wrong.   **True   False**

i) Amy — 'You can use carbon dating to find the age of any old coins you dig up.' ☐ ☐

ii) Katherine — 'Only if they're younger than 11 460 years. That's two half-lives. After that they have no carbon-14 left so they don't change any more.' ☐ ☐

iii) Laurence — 'If you use a computer to cut out experimental errors you can get the age spot-on every time.' ☐ ☐

b) For each statement that was wrong, explain why.

....

....

....

....

....

....

Radioactivity Safety

Q1   Two scientists are handling samples of radioactive material.

a)   One of the scientists is taking sensible safety precautions, but the other is not.
Describe three things which the careless scientist is doing wrong.

1. ....

2. ....

3. ....

b)   Describe another way the scientists can reduce their exposure to the radiation,
without using special apparatus or clothing.

....

c)   How should radioactive samples be stored when they are not in use?

....

Q2   The three different types of radiation can all be dangerous.

a)   Which **two** types of radiation can pass through the human body?
Circle the correct answers.

  alpha   beta   gamma

b)   **i)**   Which type of radiation is usually most dangerous if it's inhaled or swallowed?

....

   ii)   What effects can this type of radiation have on the human body?

....

....

....

Top Tips: You should always handle radioactive sources really carefully. People who work
with radioisotopes often wear **dosimeters** — badges which record their exposure. We're all exposed
to a low level of **background radiation** every day, though — from rocks etc. — and you can't do
anything about that (unless you fancy wearing a lead-lined suit and breathing apparatus all day long).

Splitting the Atom

Q1 Choose from the words below to complete the following passage.
You may need to use some words more than once.

| chemical | energy | relativity | fission | mass | equivalence | fusion |

In his theory of special ...., Einstein suggested that .... is

a form of ...., which can be converted into other forms of energy. This is

known as the principle of mass-energy .... Over 30 years later he was

proved right with the development of nuclear .... When a nucleus splits,

some of the .... is converted into a huge amount of ....

— much more than you would expect from a .... process.

Q2 Nuclear power is an example of how nuclear fission can be used **peacefully**.

a) Give one **destructive** use of nuclear fission. ....

b) How is the chain reaction different in this case compared to in a reactor?

....

Q3 Many nuclear power stations split **uranium** nuclei in their reactors.

a) Why are slow-moving neutrons fired at the uranium nuclei?

....

b) Each time a uranium atom splits, two or three neutrons are produced.
Describe how this leads to a chain reaction.

....

....

Q4 The **daughter nuclei** produced by fission are themselves **radioactive**.

a) What do the daughter nuclei do to become more stable?

....

b) Complete the following decay series for ^{91}**Kr**.

^{91}**Kr** $\Longrightarrow$ .... $\Longrightarrow$ .... $\Longrightarrow$ .... $\Longrightarrow$ ^{91}**Zr**

Nuclear Power

Q1 The diagram below shows how energy from a gas-cooled nuclear reactor generates electricity.

a) Describe how heat energy from the reactor is used to generate electricity.

....

....

b) What causes the reactor to get hot?

....

c) i) Explain how the control rods control the rate of fission.

....

....

ii) What material are control rods usually made from? ....

Q2 The majority of the UK's electricity is still produced by burning **fossil fuels**.

a) Write down one advantage and one disadvantage of nuclear power compared to using fossil fuels to generate electricity.

Advantage ....

Disadvantage ....

b) Describe how building a nuclear power plant can have a positive impact on its surrounding area.

....

Q3 **Radioactive waste** left over from **nuclear fission** is very difficult to dispose of.

a) Why is the waste produced by nuclear power stations such a long-term problem?

....

b) Describe one way of disposing of radioactive waste.

....

....

Nuclear Fusion

Q1 Decide whether the following statements are **true** or **false**.
Write out the correct version of any false statements.

		True	False

a) Nuclear fusion involves small nuclei joining together.

b) A nuclear fission reaction releases more energy than a nuclear fusion reaction.

c) Fusion reactors produce lots of radioactive waste.

d) Only a few experimental fusion reactors are generating electricity.

....

....

....

Q2 The energy released in stars comes from fusion.

a) Write down two conditions needed for fusion to take place.

1. .... 2. ....

b) Fusion reactors like JET are extremely hard to build.

i) Why can the hydrogen used not be held in a physical container?

....

ii) How do fusion reactors get around this problem?

....

c) Describe the main problem with the amount of energy a fusion reactor needs to operate.

....

Q3 In 1989 two scientists claimed to have created energy through **cold fusion**.

a) In what ways did they say cold fusion was different from previous ideas about nuclear fusion?

....

b) Suggest a reason why the report caused such excitement.

....

c) Explain why some scientists accepted the idea of cold fusion whilst others didn't.

....

....

Static Electricity

Q1 Fill in the **gaps** in these sentences with the words below.

electrons	positive	static	friction	insulating	negative

.... electricity can build up when two .... materials

are rubbed together. The .... moves .... from one

material onto the other. This leaves a .... charge on one of the

materials and a .... charge on the other.

Q2 **Circle** the pairs of charges that would attract each other and **underline** those that would repel.

positive and positive   positive and negative   negative and positive   negative and negative

Q3 The sentences below are wrong. Write out a **correct** version for each.

a) A polythene rod becomes negatively charged when rubbed with a duster because it loses electrons.

....

....

b) A charged polythene rod will repel small pieces of positively charged paper if they are placed near it.

....

....

c) The closer two charged objects are together, the less strongly they attract or repel.

....

....

d) If a positively charged object is connected to earth by a metal strap, electrons flow through the strap from the object to the ground, and the object is safely discharged.

....

....

e) Build-up of static can cause sparks if the distance between the object and the earth is big enough.

....

....

Static Electricity

Q4 A **Van de Graaff generator** is a machine which is used to generate static electricity. One type of Van de Graaff generator works like this:

1. The bottom comb is positively charged and attracts electrons away from the rubber belt.

2. The rubber belt loses electrons and becomes positively charged.

3. As the positive charge on the belt passes the top comb, electrons are attracted from the metal dome onto the belt.

4. The dome loses electrons and builds up a positive charge.

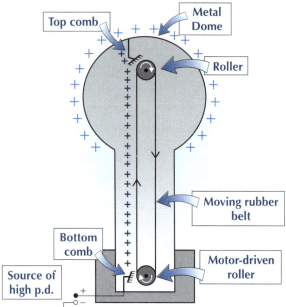

a) The top comb needs to be a **conductor**. Explain why.

....

....

b) Nadia is doing an experiment with a Van de Graaff generator. Her teacher tells her that if she touches the generator, she will become charged. When Nadia touches the generator, her hair starts to stand on end.

Use your knowledge of electrostatic charges to **explain why** Nadia's hair stands on end.

....

....

Q5 As Peter switched off his TV, he noticed that the screen was dusty. When he wiped it with his finger he heard a **crackling** sound and felt a slight **electric shock**.

Peter made two statements about what happened. Give a **reason** why he said each of the following:

a) *"The screen must have been at a high voltage."*

....

....

b) *"When I touched it, part of the screen was discharged to earth."*

....

....

Top Tips: In the exam, remember to talk about electrons flowing from one place to another. The positive charges don't move — static electricity is always due to the movement of **electrons**.

Static Electricity — Examples

Q1 Forensic scientists use an **electrostatic dust-lifter** to take fingerprints at a crime scene.

a) Use the number boxes to put the following list into the right order.

[ ] Dust particles are attracted to the thin film.

[ ] A thin film is given a high positive charge.

[1] Fine dust is brushed over the fingerprint.

[ ] The thin film is pressed onto the fingerprint.

[ ] An impression of the fingerprint is left on the film.

b) Write down two other uses for an electrostatic dust-lifter.

1. .... 2. ....

Q2 Use the words below to fill in the gaps.

fuel	earth	fuel tanker	sparks	explosion	metal strap

Static electricity can be dangerous when refuelling aircraft. If too much static builds up, there

might be ...., which can set fire to the ....

This could lead to a huge .... To prevent this happening, the fuel tank

can be connected to .... with a .... so that the

charge is conducted away. Alternatively, connect the .... to the plane.

Q3 Match up these phrases to describe what happens in a **thunderstorm**.
Write out your complete sentences below in the correct order.

If the voltage gets big enough...

... the voltage gets higher and higher.

The bottoms of the clouds become negatively charged...

... and electrons are transferred between them.

As the charge increases...

... there is a huge spark (a flash of lightning).

Raindrops and ice bump together...

... because they gain extra electrons.

1. ....

2. ....

3. ....

4. ....

94

Static Electricity — Examples

Q4 All of these statements about laser printing are wrong. Write a **corrected version** of each.

a) Under the control of a computer, the laser scans across the uncharged rotating drum and gives parts of it a positive charge, creating an image on the drum.

....
....
....

b) The toner used in a laser printer is not charged, so it will only stick to parts of the drum which are positively charged.

....
....

c) The drum rolls over an uncharged piece of paper, and the powder is attracted to the paper which picks up the image.

....
....
....

d) The paper then passes through the fuser which presses the image firmly into the paper making a permanent print.

....
....

Q5 Three friends are talking about **static electricity**.

Why do some of my clothes get charged up during the day?

Do cotton clothes get charged as much as nylon clothes?

How come I get zapped by my car door every time I get out?

Lisa

Tim

Sara

Answer their questions in the spaces below.

Lisa: ....
....

Sara: ....
....

Tim: ....
....

Top Tips: Static electricity's responsible for many of life's little annoyances — bad hair days, and those little shocks you get from touching car doors and even stroking the cat. Still, it has its uses too — the main ones you need to know about are **fingerprinting** and **laser printing**.

Mixed Questions — P2 Topics 11 & 12

Q1 The table gives information about four different **radioisotopes**.

a) Explain how the atomic structure of cobalt-60 is different from the structure of 'normal' cobalt-59.

Source	Type of Radiation	Half-life
radon-222	alpha	3.8 days
technetium-99m	gamma	6 hours
americium-241	alpha	432 years
cobalt-60	beta and gamma	5.27 years

....

....

b) Which sources in the table would be most suitable for each of the uses below?

      medical tracers   **smoke detectors**   **detecting leaks in pipes**

....

c) Radiation can be used to treat cancer.

   i) What type of radiation is used in this treatment? ....

   ii) Explain why patients often feel very ill while receiving this treatment.

      ....

d) Jim measures the count rate of a sample of americium-241 as 120 cpm.
Roughly how long would it take for the count rate to fall below **4 cpm**? Show your working.

....

....

e) Give one precaution Jim should take while handling the radioactive sample.

....

Q2 Approximately **one in 10 000 000** of the carbon atoms found in living plants or animals are atoms of the radioactive isotope **carbon-14**. After a plant or animal dies this proportion starts to decrease. Carbon-14 has a **half-life** of **5730** years.

a) Calculate the fraction of the atoms in a pure sample of carbon-14 that will still **not** have decayed after 10 half-lives have gone by.

....

....

b) Approximately how old is a bone fragment in which the proportion of carbon-14 is one part in 50 000 000? Explain your answer.

....

....

96

Mixed Questions — P2 Topics 11 & 12

Q3 The diagram below shows part of a chain reaction in a nuclear reactor.

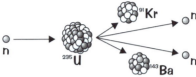

a) What is the name of the type of radioactive decay shown in the diagram? ....

b) This decay happens as part of a chain reaction. Describe what happens in this chain reaction.

....

....

c) The daughter nuclei produced are radioactive.

   i) Describe how they become stable.

   ....

   ii) Write down the decay series for ^{143}Ba.

   ....

d) How is the rate of the chain reaction controlled in a reactor?

....

e) What would happen if this reaction was not controlled?

....

f) Describe how thermal energy from the reactor is used to generate electricity.

....

....

g) Give one disadvantage of using nuclear power compared to using fossil fuels.

....

Nuclear **fusion** produces more energy than the process above.

h) i) Write down one of the conditions needed for fusion to take place.

   ....

   ii) Some scientists claim to have produced energy through cold fusion.
   Explain why the theory has not been accepted by the scientific community.

   ....

   ....

P2 Topic 12 — Power of the Atom

Mixed Questions — P2 Topics 11 & 12

Q4 The diagram shows an aircraft being refuelled.
No safety precautions have been taken.

a) **i)** Explain how static electricity could cause an explosion in this situation.

....

....

ii) Give one precaution that can be taken to avoid this danger.

....

b) Write down one example of how static electricity is **useful**.

....

Q5 Fay measures the count rate of a sample of pure copper-64 in her home, using a Geiger counter. The graph below shows her results.

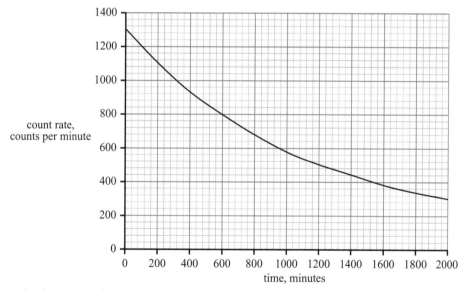

a) Fay had previously measured the background rate to be 100 counts per minute.
Find the half-life of copper-64.

....

b) She takes her Geiger counter to her friend's house and finds the background rate is much higher.
Give one reason why background radiation changes from place to place.

....

c) Her friend explains that she lives in a high **radon** area.

i) What disease is her friend more at risk of developing? ....

ii) How could she reduce the concentration of radon in her house?

....

P2 Topic 12 — Power of the Atom

Kinetic Theory and Temperature in Gases

Q1 Complete the following paragraph by choosing words from the box below.

| 0 °C | ice | 0 K | 100 °C | −273 °C | absolute | water |

The Celsius temperature scale has two fixed points. One is the melting point of ....

at .... The other is the boiling point of .... at ....

The lowest fixed point on the kelvin temperature scale is at the lowest temperature possible

— called .... zero. This is given a value of .... and it is

equivalent to a temperature on the Celsius scale of about ....

Q2 Complete the following sentences by choosing the correct word from each pair.

a) At 0 **°C** / **K** the internal energy of any substance is at its lowest possible value.

b) When a gas is heated, the particles in it move **faster** / **more slowly**.

c) The average **kinetic** / **potential** energy of particles in a gas is **equal** / **proportional** to the temperature of the gas on the kelvin scale.

Q3 Convert the following temperatures to **kelvin** (K).

a) 3 °C ....

b) 210 °C ....

c) −45 °C ....

d) 0 °C ....

Q4 Convert the following temperatures to **°C**.

a) 0 K ....

b) 300 K ....

c) 640 K ....

d) 30 K ....

Q5 The kinetic energy of particles depends on their mass and their velocity.

a) What is the **formula** for the kinetic energy of a particle of mass **m** travelling at velocity **v**?

....

b) The temperature of a gas is increased from 277 °C to 827 °C. At 277 °C the mean kinetic energy of the gas is 1.14×10^{20} joules. What is it at 827 °C?

Always start a kinetic theory question involving temperature by converting degrees celsius to kelvin.

....

....

c) Explain why it takes longer for the smell of air freshener to spread through a room on a cold day than on a hot day.

....

Kinetic Theory and Pressure in Gases

Q1 **Kinetic theory** can be used to explain the behaviour and properties of gases.

a) What does kinetic theory say that a gas consists of? Choose **two** options from A to E below.

    A stationary particles   **B** very small particles   **C** a rigid mesh of particles

    D mostly empty space   **E** fluctuations in electric and magnetic fields

b) Explain how the impact of gas molecules on the sides of a container relates to the pressure of a gas.

....

....

Q2 The apparatus shown in the diagram can be used to show how **pressure** changes with **temperature** for a gas.

a) What variable is kept constant by having the gas in a rigid sealed container? Circle the correct letter.

    A Pressure   **B** Volume   **C** Temperature

b) On the graph below, point A shows the pressure and temperature of the gas when an experiment began. Point B is the point at which the gas could not be heated any more with this apparatus. Explain why B occurs at a temperature of 100 °C.

....

....

c) On the graph, continue the line to show how an ideal gas would behave if it was **cooled** to absolute zero.

d) At what temperature in degrees celsius would the pressure be **zero**?

....

Q3 A bubble of carbon dioxide leaves a plant at the bottom of a lake. Initially it has a volume of **5 cm³** and is at a pressure of **6 atm**. The temperature at the bottom of the lake is **4 °C**. The bubble rises and just before it reaches the surface it is at a pressure of **1 atm** and a temperature of **20 °C**.

a) Give two reasons why the volume of the bubble will **increase** as it rises.

1. ....

2. ....

b) Calculate the **volume** of the bubble just before it reaches the surface.

Don't forget to convert temperatures to kelvin.

....

....

Particles in Atoms

Q1 Alpha, beta and gamma are all types of ionising radiation, but they have quite different properties.

a) Rate the different types of radiation according to their penetrating power.

> 1 = high penetrating power
>
> 2 = moderate penetrating power
>
> 3 = low penetrating power

alpha ☐   gamma ☐

beta ☐

b) How does the **penetrating power** of each type of radiation compare to its **ionising power**?

....

c) Give an example of a material that can stop

i) **alpha** radiation ....   ii) **beta** radiation ....

Q2 Complete the following sentences about **radioactive decay**.

a) During α decay, the nucleus loses .... protons and .... neutrons.

So its mass number decreases by .... and its atomic number decreases by ....

b) During β⁻ decay a .... becomes a .... The atomic number

increases by 1 and the mass number ....

c) During β⁺ decay a .... becomes a .... The atomic number

.... and the mass number stays the same.

d) α, β⁺ or β⁻ decay results in the formation of a different ...., which is shown

by the change in .... number.

e) When a nucleus emits a γ ray, its mass number changes by .... and its atomic

number changes by ....

Q3 Neutrons are found in the nuclei of atoms and can also be emitted as a form of radiation. Underline the correct words from the options given.

a) Neutron radiation is **more** / **less** penetrating than alpha or beta radiation.

b) Neutrons do not have electric **charge** / **power** so they do not directly **absorb** / **ionise** material they pass through.

c) Absorbing a neutron can make a nucleus **ionised** / **radioactive**.

Particles in Atoms

Q4 The equation shows an isotope of carbon undergoing radioactive decay.

a) What type of radioactive decay is this?

....

$$^{14}_{6}C \longrightarrow X + ^{0}_{+1}e$$

b) Give the **nucleon number** and **atomic number** of element X.

nucleon number: .... atomic number: ....

c) People take precautions against cell damage from ionisation by most types of radiation. Why is it not necessary to take particular precautions against this type of radiation?

....

Q5 The graph on the right shows the number of neutrons (N) against the number of protons (Z) for **stable isotopes**.

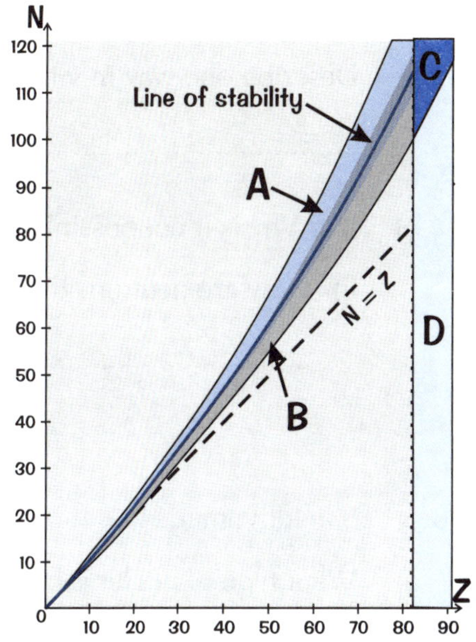

a) What are **isotopes** of an element?

....

....

b) Are isotopes in region A stable or unstable? Circle your answer.

    stable   unstable

c) Are isotopes in region A neutron-rich or proton-rich?

    neutron-rich   proton-rich

d) Suggest a reason why isotopes in region B are **unstable**.

....

e) In order to achieve stability, what type of decay will isotopes in **region B** undergo?

....

f) What type of decay will isotopes in **region C** undergo in order to achieve stability?

....

g) What type of particle will isotopes in **region D** emit in order to become more stable?

....

Particles in Atoms

Q6   **Alpha particles** are strongly ionising.

a)   What kinds of atom undergo alpha decay?

....

b)   Circle the two of these elements that undergo alpha decay.   H   U   Th   C   He

c)   Complete this nuclear equation.

$$^{224}_{88}\text{Ra} \longrightarrow \boxed{}\text{Rn} + \boxed{}\text{alpha}$$

d)   After alpha (or beta) decay, a nucleus often has too much energy. How does it lose this energy?

....

Q7   Neutrons are very difficult to detect.

a)   Describe one way in which electrons can be detected.

....

b)   **i)**   Why is it not possible to detect neutrons in this way? ....

　　　　ii)   How are neutrons detected?

　　　　...

Q8   Shielding made of **concrete** can be used as protection against neutron radiation.

a)   What type of nuclei is best for absorbing neutron radiation? ....

b)   Explain how the shielding works.

....

....

c)   Concrete shielding alone is not enough to prevent the harmful effects of neutron radiation.
　　　　Explain why.

....

....

d)   Write down an example of a material that could be added
　　　　to the shielding to stop any radiation getting through.

....

Fundamental and Other Particles

Q1   Many particles can be split into even smaller particles.

a)   What is a **fundamental particle**?

....

b)   Which of the following are fundamental particles?

Proton	Electron	Neutron	Monkey	Positron	Alpha particle

c)   Can new fundamental particles ever be created? How?

....

Q2   Tick the statements that are **true**.

a)   Quarks are made up of protons and neutrons.   ☐

b)   The relative mass of a quark is 1/3.   ☐

c)   All quarks have the same charge.   ☐

d)   There are 2 quarks in a proton.   ☐

e)   There are 2 types of quark in a neutron.   ☐

quark quark

Q3   Match the **particles** on the left with the correct description of their properties.

Electron

Down-quark

Proton

Neutron

Positron

Up-quark

relative mass 1/3, relative charge 2/3

relative mass 1, charge +1

fundamental particle, charge −1

relative charge −1/3

made up of two down-quarks and one up-quark

fundamental particle, charge +1

Q4   The number of protons and neutrons in a nucleus can make it **unstable**.

a)   Complete the following sentence.

To become more stable, the nucleus can convert a neutron into a ....

b)   What particle must be emitted to keep the overall charge zero? ....

c)   What is this process called? ....

Fundamental and Other Particles

Q5 Scientists at CERN carry out experiments involving smashing particles together at high speed.

a) Fill in the **gaps** in this passage.

> In an experiment, two protons are .... to very high speed and
>
> made to collide. The collision produces a large amount of ....
>
> Some of this .... can be turned into mass. The mass created is
>
> equal parts .... and anti... .

b) Antimatter is made up of antiparticles

   i) Give one **similarity** between a particle and its antiparticle. ....

   ii) Give one **difference** between a particle and its antiparticle. ....

   iii) Name the antiparticle of the electron. ....

c) The **antiproton** is the antiparticle of the proton. Is the antiproton a fundamental particle?
Explain your answer.

   ....

d) What is the relative **charge** on an antiproton? ....

Q6 The charges on protons and neutrons are determined by the quarks that form them.

a) Make simple sketch diagrams of a **proton** and a **neutron**, showing the number and type of quarks
each contains.

Proton	Neutron

b) Complete the blanks in this sentence:

   In beta decay, a proton is converted to a .... and a .... is emitted.

c) Describe β+ **decay** in terms of what happens to the quarks in a proton.

   ....

Top Tips: Everything, everywhere is made of particles — make sure you know each type,
their charge and mass. Learn which are fundamental, and how they go together to make the rest.

Electron Beams

Q1   The diagram shows an **electron gun**.

a)   Use the following words to fill in the labels on the diagram. Words may be used more than once.

vacuum
heater
electrons
anode
deflecting
cathode

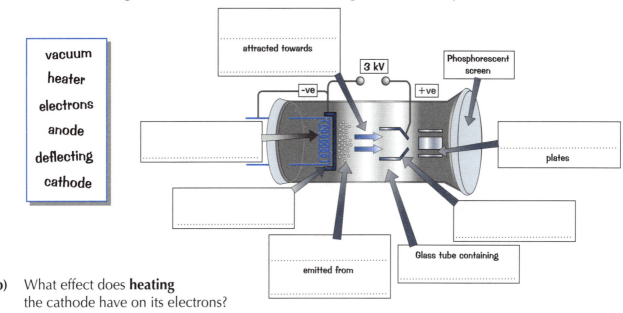

attracted towards

3 kV

-ve

+ve

Phosphorescent screen

plates

Glass tube containing

emitted from

b)   What effect does **heating** the cathode have on its electrons?

....

c)   Which components in the electron gun use electric fields to make electrons change:

i)   speed? ....

ii)   direction? ....

d)   What happens when an electron hits the phosphorescent screen?

....

Q2   A beam of electrons leaves an **electron gun**. The current carried by the beam is 4 mA.

a)   What is current a measure of?

....

b)   How many **coulombs** of charge pass a certain point in the beam per second?

....

c)   How many **electrons** pass this point per second?

....

The charge on an electron is -1.6×10^{-19} C.

Q3   The electron beam in a cathode ray tube is deflected by an **electric field** between two pairs of charged metal plates. Circle the correct words from each pair to complete the following sentences.

a)   The electron beam is **attracted to** / **repelled by** a positive charge and **attracted to** / **repelled by** a negative charge.

b)   The **Y-plates** / **X-plates** deflect the beam up and down, while the **Y-plates** / **X-plates** deflect the beam left and right.

Electron Beams

Q4   An **electron** accelerates across a potential difference (voltage) of 4 kV.
The charge on the electron is –1.6 × 10⁻¹⁹ C.

a)   Calculate the **kinetic energy** gained by the electron.

....

b)   How much **potential energy** will the electron lose?

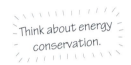
Think about energy conservation.

....

Q5   The diagram below shows the screen of an **oscilloscope**. The position of the spot of light is
controlled by charged metal plates that **deflect** the beam of electrons from the cathode ray tube.

The dot shows the position of the electron beam when a positive potential is connected to X1 and
Y1, so X1 is more positive than X2 and Y1 is more positive than Y2.

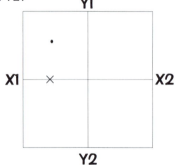

a)   Draw in the position of the electron beam if the connections
to X1 and X2 are swapped round so that a positive potential
is connected to X2 and Y1.

b)   Sketch the path of the electron beam from the point marked
with a cross, as the following voltage changes occur:

   i)   The positive potential of X2 is increased while the
positive potential of Y2 is also increased.

   ii)   When the potentials of X1 and X2 are equal, the positive potential of Y2 is decreased,
while the positive potential of X2 continues to increase.

   iii)   The voltage changes stop when the potentials of Y1 and Y2 are equal.
At this point X2 is more positive than X1.

Q6   The diagram below shows a machine for taking **dental X-rays**.

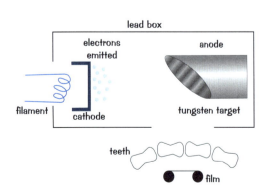

a)   Sketch in and label the **path of the electron beam**
on the diagram. Show the direction of the beam.

b)   Sketch in and label the **path of the X-rays** on the
diagram. Show the direction of the beam.

c)   Why does the **electron beam** move from cathode
to the anode?

....

....

d)   At the **anode** the electrons from the beam strike atoms of tungsten, causing them to emit **X-rays**.
Where does the energy for the X-rays come from?

....

Electron Beams

Q7 Scientists at CERN use an enormous **particle accelerator** to smash particles into each other at tremendous speeds.

a) How are particle accelerators such as the one at CERN similar to electron guns?

....

The beams of charged particles in particle accelerators are deflected by charged metal plates in the same way as the beam of electrons in an electron gun.

b) When the factors below are **increased** will the deflection of a beam of charged particles increase, decrease or remain unchanged? Connect each factor with its effect on the deflection.

charge on the plates   increase   mass of the particles

mass of the plates   decrease

charge on the particles   no change   speed of the particles

c) Give two reasons why scientists from all over Europe collaborate on the research at CERN.

....

....

Q8 Laurence and Amy are experimenting with an **electron gun** similar to the one in question 1. They connect the anode and cathode with a wire containing an ammeter, as shown below.

a) The ammeter shows that a current is flowing even though there appears to be a gap in the circuit between the cathode and the anode. Describe how the circuit has been completed.

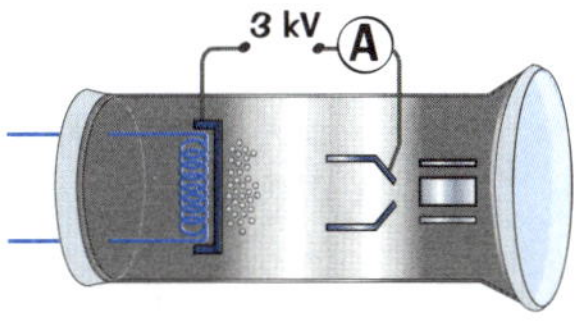

....

....

b) Laurence connects the positive terminal of a battery to the upper deflection plate, and the negative terminal of the battery to the lower deflection plate.

i) What happens to the plates?

....

ii) What happens to the electron beam?

....

iii) What do they see on the phosphorescent screen?

....

c) Give a common 'household' use of electron guns. ....

Mixed Questions — P3 Topic 5

Q1 When **high-energy** electrons are fired at protons and neutrons the deflection of the electrons shows that both protons and neutrons are made up of charged particles called **quarks**.

a) Describe the types of quark found in protons and neutrons, include their relative charge and mass.

  i) up-quarks: ....

  ii) down-quarks: ....

b) Why do electrons **change direction** when they come near quarks?

  ....

Q2 Anna is investigating the properties of stable and unstable isotopes. She fires neutrons at a stable isotope of carbon. The isotope **absorbs a neutron** and becomes unstable. Anna adds the unstable isotope to a graph showing the number of neutrons and the number of protons in stable isotopes.

a) Would you expect the unstable carbon isotope to lie above, below or on the line of stability on the graph? Give a reason for your answer.

  ....

b) **i)** Complete the following equation describing the decay of the isotope: $^{13}_{6}C \longrightarrow \boxed{}N + ^{0}_{-1}e$

  ii) What is this sort of decay called? ....

c) Describe the decay in terms of what happens to the **quarks** in a neutron within the isotope's nucleus.

  ....

d) The isotope is still unstable because it has too much **energy**. How can the isotope become stable?

  ....

Q3 A container of gas has a pressure of 1×10^5 N/m² and a volume of **100 cm³**.

a) The volume of the gas is gradually increased while the temperature remains constant. Calculate the **pressure** of the gas at the following volumes.

  i) 200 cm³ ....

  ii) 400 cm³ ....

b) When the pressure of the gas is 1.25×10^4 N/m², what will its **volume** be?

  ....

  ....

c) On the grid opposite, draw a **graph** showing how pressure varies against volume at constant temperature for this gas.

Mixed Questions — P3 Topic 5

Q4 **Electron guns** are made up of many parts, each with its own specific function.

a) Draw lines to connect each part of the electron gun with its function.

X-plates

Deflection along a horizontal axis

Anode

Heats the cathode

Heater

Deflection along a vertical axis

Y-plates

Accelerates the electron beam

b) i) What is **thermionic emission**? ....

ii) Where in an electron gun does it occur? ....

A beam of electrons passes through an electric field generated by a pair
of vertical deflector plates. The top plate is connected to the positive terminal
of a battery, and the bottom plate is connected to the negative terminal.

upper deflector plate
▭ +

beam of particles →

▭ −
lower deflector plate

c) On the diagram, sketch the path the beam of electrons
will take through the deflector plates.

d) Draw and label the paths you would expect a beam of the
following particles to take through the deflector plates:

i) neutrons

ii) protons

e) It took 40 years from the discovery of protons and electrons for the neutron to be detected.
Suggest a reason why the neutron was discovered so much later.

....

Q5 The gas inside a rigid, **sealed** container is cooled from 527 °C to –73 °C.

a) Convert these temperatures to kelvin:

i) 527 °C = ... K

ii) –73 °C = ... K

b) What will happen to:

i) the average **kinetic energy** of the gas particles? ....

ii) the average **speed** of the gas particles? ....

iii) the average **force** exerted on the walls of the container? ....

c) Use **kinetic theory** to explain how the pressure of a gas depends on the movement of particles.

....

....

d) What is the mathematical relationship between the kinetic energy and temperature of a gas?

....

Mixed Questions — Topic 5

Q6 The **electron-volt (eV)** is the amount of kinetic energy gained by one electron when it moves through a potential difference of one volt.

a) The charge on an electron is -1.6×10^{-19} C. What is the value, in joules, of 1 eV?

....

b) Complete the blanks in the following passage:

Particle accelerators are used to make particles .... with each other at

high speed, releasing .... In some cases this ....

turns into ...., creating a particle / antiparticle pair.

c) Why do physicists sometimes measure the mass of particles in eV?

....

d) Apart from particle accelerators, suggest one other **scientific** use of electron guns.

....

Q7 Choose the correct **particle** or particles for each of the descriptions below. The same option may be used once, more than once or not at all.

protons   neutrons   ions   electrons   positrons

a) can make up an electric current ....

b) are fundamental particles ....

c) are released in beta-plus decay ....

d) are made up of three quarks ....

Q8 Radon gas is a source of background radiation that occurs naturally in the air.

a) The following incomplete equation shows the decay of radon gas to solid polonium. $^{222}_{86}\text{Rn} \longrightarrow \square_\square\text{Po} + \square_\square$ ....

   i) What sort of decay would you expect radon to undergo? Give a reason for your answer.

....

   ii) Complete the equation.

b) A rigid, sealed container of radon gas at a pressure of 101 kPa is heated from 273 K to 293 K. Calculate the pressure at the new temperature. Assume the radon behaves as an ideal gas.

....

....

Total Internal Reflection

Q1 The diagram shows light entering a glass block. Light travels **more slowly** in **glass** than in air.

Complete the diagram to show the ray passing through the block and emerging from the other side. Include labels A to E for:

    A   the refracted ray

    B   the emergent ray

    C   the normal for the emergent ray

    D   the angle of incidence

    E   the angle of refraction

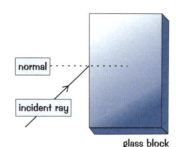

glass block

Q2 Choose from the words below to complete the passage.

pulses	thousands	reflected	internal	diffraction	dense	core	infrared	gamma

Optical fibres depend on total .... reflection for their operation.

Visible light or .... waves are sent down the cable and are

.... when they hit the boundary between the .... of the

fibre and the less .... outer case. The signals travel as ....

of light. Each cable can carry .... of different signals.

Q3 Tick to show whether these statements are **true** or **false**.

                                                                                       True False

  a) For the signal to be transmitted, the rays must not enter the fibre at too sharp an angle. ☐ ☐

  b) Optical fibres are subject to interference from other signals. ☐ ☐

Q4 The diagrams show rays of light in an **optical fibre**.
Draw arrows to match each diagram to the correct description of what is happening.

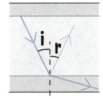
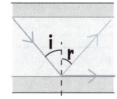
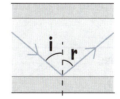

Total internal reflection

Most of the light passes out of the optical fibre, but some is reflected internally.

Most of the light is reflected internally, but some emerges along the surface of the glass.

Q5 What is meant by the '**critical angle**' for a material?

....

....

Medical Uses of Light

Q1 The diagram below shows a **pulse oximeter** on a hospital patient's **finger**.

a) Add arrows to the diagram to show the direction of the red light and infrared beams.

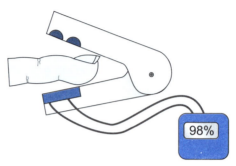

b) Choose from the words given below to complete the passage about how a pulse oximeter works.

reflected	reduced	absorbed	calibrated	monkey	tissue	increased

Red and infrared light pass through the .... and are detected by a photo detector. Some of the light is .... by the red blood so that the amount of light detected by the detector is .... The amount of light absorbed depends on the amount of oxyhaemoglobin in the blood so the display can be .... to show the blood's oxyhaemoglobin content.

c) State one other suitable part of the **body** where a pulse oximeter could be placed. Explain your answer.

....

....

Q2 Optical fibres work because of repeated **total internal reflections**.

a) Complete the **ray diagrams** below. The critical angle for glass/air is **42°**.

You'll need to measure the angle of incidence for each one — carefully.

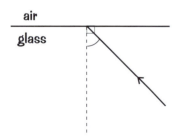
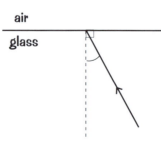
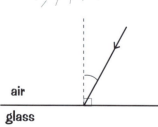

b) What two conditions are essential for **total internal reflection** to occur?

1. ....

2. ....

P3 Topic 6 — Medical Physics

Medical Uses of Light

Q3 Doctors use **endoscopes** to look inside patients' bodies. Endoscopes work using **optical fibres**.

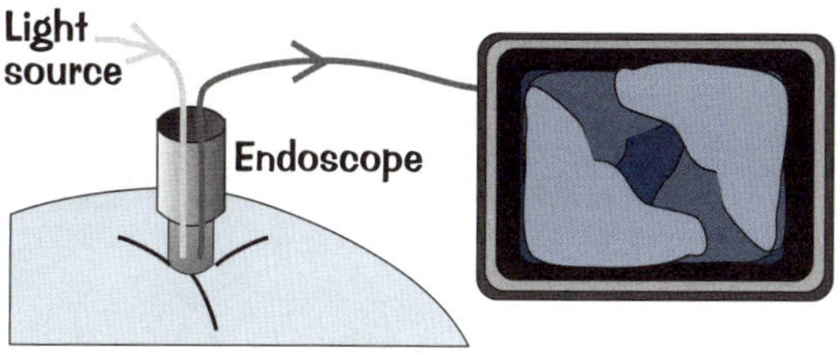

a) What **material** could the optical fibres in an endoscope be made from?

Light source

Endoscope

....

b) Explain why doctors try not to to **bend** an endoscope sharply.

....

....

Q4 The diagram shows the use of an **endoscope** in **keyhole surgery**.

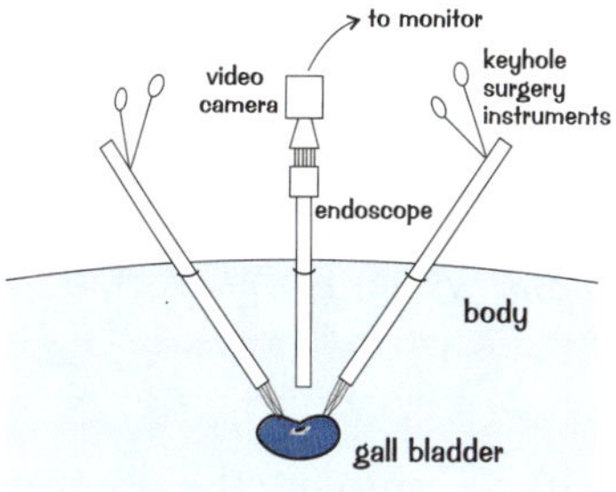

to monitor

video camera

keyhole surgery instruments

endoscope

body

gall bladder

a) Explain what is meant by the term **keyhole surgery**.

....

....

b) Outline how an **endoscope** works.

....

....

c) List two **advantages** of keyhole surgery over conventional surgery.

....

Q5 **Reflection** pulse oximetry is used to measure the amount of oxygen in the blood.

a) How does reflection pulse oximetry differ from the type of pulse oximetry described in question 1?

....

b) Connect the boxes below to complete the sentences about haemoglobin.

Oxyhaemoglobin is...

...purply coloured...

...and doesn't contain much oxygen.

Reduced haemoglobin is...

...bright red...

...and rich in oxygen.

Top Tips: When you're learning about endoscopes, impress your friends by casually dropping the word 'esophagogastroduodenoscopy' into conversation. It means using an endoscope to have a look all the way down someone's throat right to their guts – mmm, nice.

Work, Power and Energy

Q1 In his new job, John has to climb the stairs on average **6 times** every day. After doing this for six months, he finds he has lost **15 kg**.

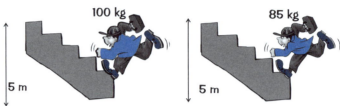

Calculate the work done by John each day in climbing the stairs:

a) When he started his new job.

....

b) Six months later, after his weight loss.

....

Q2 Kat was in a car accident and injured her left arm. Her physiotherapist gives Kat exercises to restore the power of her arm. For one exercise, Kat must **raise** a **100 N** load over **0.5 m**.

a) What is the work done by Kat in raising the load?

....

b) Complete the physiotherapist's table recording Kat's progress over four days of treatment.

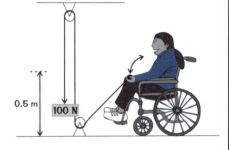

days of treatment	1	2	3	4
time taken to raise load (s)	5.0	4.0	....	1
patient's power rating (W)	10.0	....	20.0	....

c) What does Kat's changing power rating suggest about her arm?

....

d) What **further information** does the physiotherapist need if she is to decide whether or not Kat has fully recovered the power of her injured arm?

....

Q3 Isaac is stacking a **1.5 m** high shelf with **10 N** bags of sugar from the floor.

a) Calculate how much **energy** Isaac **transfers** to each bag.

....

b) Calculate how much **work** Isaac does when he stacks 20 bags of sugar.

....

c) Is work a type of energy? Explain your answer.

....

Work, Power and Energy

Q4 Tim is canoeing down a stretch of river. Tim's mass is **73 kg** and his canoe weighs **190 N**.

a) The river is flowing at 1.3 m/s. Tim starts off with the same speed as the river then paddles hard, accelerating to 4.4 m/s over 5 s. Calculate his acceleration.

....

b) Tim accelerates at this rate over a distance of 150 m.
Calculate the work done by Tim on this part of the river.

....

....

Q5 Farmer Ted's horse can pull a load of **1000 N** over **20 m** in **25 s**.

a) Calculate the power of Farmer Ted's horse.

....

b) When he is not pulling a load, Farmer Ted's horse can run at 13 m/s. The mass of the horse is 800 kg. Calculate the **kinetic energy** gained by the horse when it accelerates from 0 to 13 m/s.

....

c) Calculate the power, in **watts**, of the horse when it runs at 13 m/s for 90 s.

....

d) Suggest a reason why the horse's power is lower in your second calculation.

....

Q6 Fiona is a weightlifter. She lifts a **70 kg barbell** from the floor to above her head, so it is **2.1 m** above the ground.

$g = 10 \, m/s^2$

a) How much potential energy has Fiona transferred to the barbell?

....

b) If Fiona takes 5 s to lift the barbell how powerful is she?

....

c) Fiona attempts to lift an 80 kg barbell. It takes her 5 s to get it to 1.9 m above the ground, but she cannot lift it any further, so drops the barbell to the floor.

i) Calculate the power Fiona used in this lift.

....

ii) Calculate the maximum velocity reached by the barbell as it falls. Ignore air resistance.

....

Energy and Metabolic Rate

Q1 The table shows some activities and the **metabolic rates** associated with them.

a) What does metabolic rate mean?

....

....

b) Complete the table by inserting a suitable metabolic rate for **watching TV**.

Activity	kJ/min
Sleeping	4.5
Watching TV	
Cycling (15 mph)	21
Jogging (5 mph)	40
Slow walking	14

c) i) Suggest three processes within a person's body that require energy while they're watching TV.

....

ii) Where does the energy for these processes come from?

....

Q2 Ed says that his metabolic rate must be lowest just after lunch because this is when he has the most trouble paying attention in lessons, so his body must be transferring energy to his brain very slowly.

a) Explain why Ed's reasoning is incorrect.

....

b) A person's lowest metabolic rate is called the **basal metabolic rate** or BMR.

i) What does BMR measure in terms of the processes going on in a person's body?

....

ii) Outline how to measure Ed's BMR and show him that his metabolic rate is higher after lunch.

....

....

....

Q3 The diagram shows Denny jogging up a hill. His metabolic rate as he jogs is **50 kJ/min**.

a) How much energy does Denny use in the 3 minutes it takes him to jog up the hill?

....

b) Calculate the potential energy Denny gains by reaching the top of the hill.

....

100 m

600 N

c) Explain why the energy used by Denny to jog up the hill is greater than the potential energy he gains at the top.

....

....

Energy and Metabolic Rate

Q4   The graph below shows how the **basal metabolic rate** of Joanna and her mum vary over time.

a)   Joanna is 6 years old and her mum is 34. Use your knowledge of how BMR varies with **age** to label the graph. Use **J** for Joanna and **M** for her mum.

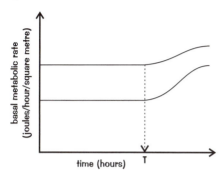

b)   The graph shows that both Joanna and her mum's BMRs began to rise at time T.

   i)   Suggest what may have happened at **time T** to cause this.

   ....

   ii)   What physical factor may have caused Joanna and her mum's BMRs to increase at different rates, as shown by the graph?

   ....

Q5   Chloe's doctor advises her that her current weight is unhealthy and she should try to lose some weight. Her friend suggests she should reduce her food consumption to 300 kcal per day.

a)   i)   Explain the effect such a dramatic reduction in energy intake would have on Chloe's BMR.

   ....

   ii)   Why would this not help Chloe lose as much weight as she might expect?

   ....

b)   Chloe's doctor tells her that reducing her energy intake this much is a really bad way to lose weight, and could be harmful. He says she should start exercising as well as changing her eating habits. Give **two** reasons why exercise can help people to lose weight.

   ....

   ....

Q6   Dr Mayer worked with patients who travelled between Europe and Indonesia in the 20th century. He realised that his patients had a lower metabolic rate when they were in Indonesia than they had in Europe.

Explain how the difference between the European and tropical Indonesian climates caused this effect.

   ....

   ....

Electricity and the Body

Q1 Sharma is in hospital to have an **electromyogram** (**EMG**) of the muscles in her legs.
The muscles have become weaker recently, her doctor thinks she may have **muscular dystrophy**.

a) What does an EMG machine measure?

....

b) Define the following terms:

i) resting potential ....

ii) action potential ....

c) What value would you expect to record from a **contracted** muscle cell in a healthy person?

....

Q2 Electrocardiographs (ECGs) are used to measure the activity of the **heart**.

a) Describe, briefly, the **structure** of the heart.

....

b) Describe how a series of electrical signals help to produce a heart beat.

....

....

c) Describe the sensors used to detect the action potentials of a patient's heart.

....

Q3 The diagram below shows a typical **ECG**.

a) Show the size of the **resting potential** with an arrow on the y-axis.

b) What is the **period** of the heartbeat? ....

c) Calculate the frequency of the heartbeat in **beats per minute.**

....

d) What **muscle action** in the heart is being recorded at points:

i) P ....

ii) QRS ....

iii) T ....

Intensity of Radiation

Q1   The word '**radiation**' is often used to refer to nuclear sources, but it also covers many other types.

a)   Sort the following forms of radiation according to their properties.

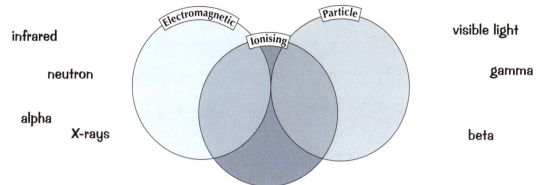

infrared

neutron

alpha

X-rays

visible light

gamma

beta

b)   What is the definition of radiation?

....

Q2   Jonny is watching Kill Phil using a projector and a screen. The bulb in his projector gives an intensity of **8 W/m²** on the projector screen in its current position.

a)   Write down the intensity of radiation on the screen if the distance between the bulb and screen is:

i)   doubled. ....

ii)   halved. ....

iii) quadrupled. ....

b)   Write down the intensity of radiation on the screen if only the power of the bulb was doubled.

....

Q3   Sam and Amy have made a spherical lantern for the halloween parade. The lantern has a **diameter** of **40 cm** and contains a candle with a power of **0.8 W** at its center.

a)   Calculate the surface area of the lantern, in square metres.

....

....

Remember the surface area of a sphere $=4/3 \pi r^2$

b)   Calculate the **intensity** of the light radiation on the inside surface of the lantern.

....

c)   How will the intensity of the light from the candle reaching the outside surface of the lantern compare to that reaching the inside surface? Explain your answer.

....

Top Tips: If this intensity of radiation malarkey is just not making sense, try getting a torch out and seeing it in action. Hold your hand up close to the torch, what do you see — a bright spot of light. Shine it on the fence at the bottom of the garden, guess what — a large patch of dim light.

Nuclear Bombardment

Q1 Uranium-235 is split in nuclear reactors to release energy. Some products of the fission can also be used for medical applications.

a) Uranium-235 must be converted to uranium-236 using a thermal neutron.

i) What is a thermal neutron?

....

ii) Describe how uranium-235 is converted into uranium-236.

....

b) U-236 splits into two smaller atoms, which are often unstable. What makes these atoms unstable?

....

c) Suggest one medical application for the products of the fission of uranium-235.

....

Q2 Bombarding stable elements with **protons** can produce **radioactive isotopes**.
Complete the following passage using the words provided.

nucleus	accelerator	cyclotron	electron	proton	element	mass

A proton is absorbed by the .... This increases its

.... number so a new .... is produced.

The proton needs a lot of energy before it can be absorbed by the nucleus, so this process

takes place in a particle .... called a ....

Q3 The radioisotopes produced by proton bombardment are **unstable**.

a) Complete the following equations to show how two radioisotopes are formed.

$$^{18}_{8}O + \, ^{1}_{1}p \longrightarrow \, ^{\square}_{\square}F + \, ^{1}_{0}n \qquad\qquad ^{14}_{7}N + \, ^{1}_{1}p \longrightarrow \, ^{\square}_{\square}C + \, ^{4}_{2}He$$

b) i) What sort of radiation do the radioisotopes formed in this way usually emit?

....

ii) Suggest a medical use for these radioisotopes.

....

iii) Explain why some hospitals have their own facilities for producing these radioisotopes.

....

<u>Momentum Conservation</u>

Q1 The diagram shows a fast moving **neutron colliding** with a stationary sodium **nucleus** and bouncing off again.

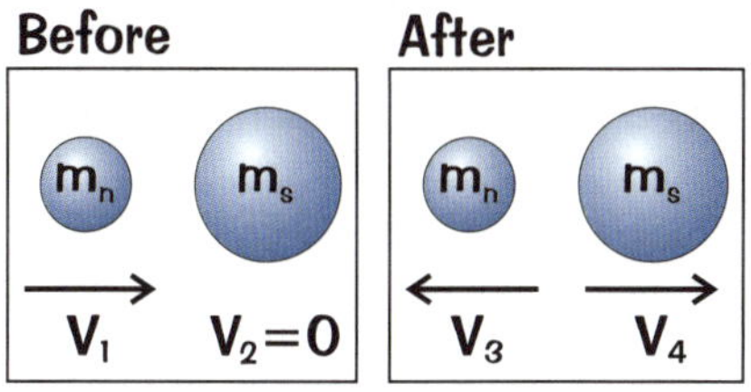

Before   **After**

a) Using the notation in the diagram, write an expression for:

    i) the total momentum before the collision.

    ....

    ii) the total momentum after the collision.

    ....

b) Using your answers to part a), explain what is meant by the term **conservation of momentum**.

....

Q2 The diagram below shows the **collision** of a neutron and an atom of uranium-235.

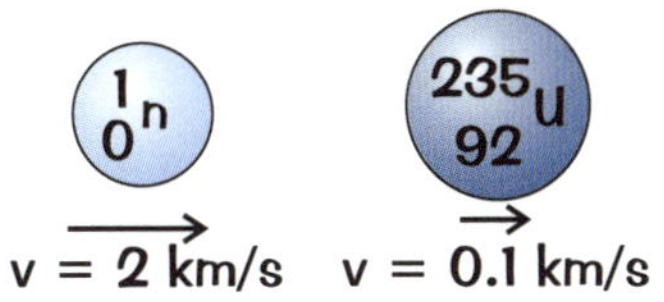

$v = 2$ km/s $v = 0.1$ km/s

Use the relative masses in your calculations.

a) Calculate the relative momentum of the:

    i) neutron. ....

    ii) uranium-235 nucleus. ....

b) The uranium-235 nucleus absorbs the neutron to form uranium-236. What is the relative momentum of the uranium-236 isotope?

....

Q3 The diagram shows the **alpha decay** of **uranium-238**.

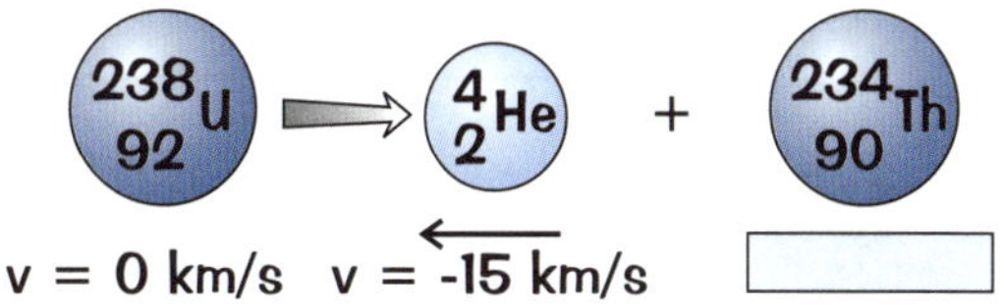

a) **i)** Add an arrow to the diagram to show which way the **thorium** nucleus will move.

    ii) Explain why it must move this way.

$v = 0$ km/s $v = -15$ km/s

....

b) Calculate the **velocity** of the thorium nucleus immediately after the decay.

....

Q4 A **proton** collides with a **stationary** isotope of **oxygen-16** and is absorbed.

a) The collision forms an isotope of fluorine with a relative mass of 17 and a velocity of 37 km/s.

    i) Calculate the relative momentum of the fluorine atom after the collision.

    ....

    ii) What was the velocity of the proton before the collision?

    ....

b) The fluorine isotope is unstable and emits an alpha particle at a velocity of −15 000 km/s. What is the velocity of the nitrogen-13 isotope formed by this decay?

....

Momentum Conservation

Q5 The diagram represents the **collision** of an **electron** and a **positron**.

electron   positron

e⁻   e⁺

→   ←

a) What is the result of a collision between a particle and its antiparticle?

....

b) The electron and positron are travelling at the same speed before the collision. What is the value of their **total momentum** immediately before the collision?

....

c) Choose the correct words from each pair to complete the sentences below.

The collision of an electron and a positron produces a pair of **gamma rays** / **radioactive particles**. The **gamma rays** / **radioactive particles** produced have the same **energy** / **velocity** as each other, and opposite **energies** / **velocities**.

d) Explain how this collision is an example of mass/energy conservation.

....

....

Q6 A proton with a velocity of -2 km/s is travelling towards an electron moving at 90 km/s.

a) In box A, sketch a diagram showing the proton and the electron just before they collide.

A	B

b) The mass of an electron is approximately 1/2000ᵗʰ the mass of a proton. Calculate the total relative momentum just before the particles collide.

....

c) Just after the collision the electron has a velocity of -3000 km/s. Calculate the velocity of the proton immediately after the collision.

....

d) In box B, draw a diagram to show the particles immediately after the collision.

Top Tips: If you know your equations, this section is the chance to earn some tasty marks without too much trouble. Learning equations isn't the most exciting job in the world — but it does pay off. Remember, things with momentum are **mo**v**ing** — and that momentum equation — m × v.

Medical Uses of Radiation

Q1   Positron emission tomography (PET) is a scanning technique used in hospitals.

   a)   Give one advantage and one disadvantage of PET compared to X-rays.

     i)   advantage: ....

     ii)   disadvantage: ....

   b)   Give two conditions that can be researched using PET.

     ....

Q2   Put the following stages in the right order to explain how PET is carried out.

   ☐   The radiotracer moves through the body to the organs.

   ☐   Detectors around the body record the position of the emitted gamma rays.

   ☐   The patient is injected with the radiotracer.

   ☐   The positrons collide with electrons and are annihilated, releasing gamma rays.

   ☐   The radioisotope emits positrons.

   [1]   A positron-emitting radioactive isotope is added to a substance used by the body to make a radio tracer.

   ☐   A computer builds up a map of radioactivity in the body.

Q3   The **map of radioactivity** in the body produced by a PET scan can be used to detect active cancer tumors.

   a)   **i)**   What does the map of radioactivity match up with?

        ....

     ii)   Why is this?

        ....

   b)   Explain why a PET scan is a good way to detect cancer.

     ....

   c)   Why is PET not used frequently on the same patient?

     ....

Q4   **Radiation exposure** can be damaging, but is also used as a medical treatment.

   a)   Explain how radiotherapy can be used as a form of **palliative care**.

     ....

     ....

   b)   Describe **two** ways that radiation can damage cells.

     ....

Medical Research

Q1 Draw lines to match each medical **technique** on the left to the medical **condition** or process each might be used in.

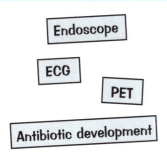

Endoscope

ECG

PET

Antibiotic development

Keyhole surgery

Monitoring heart conditions

Mutating bacteria ('superbugs')

Locating cancer cells

Q2 Read the paragraph below and outline an argument **for** and an argument **against embryonic stem cell harvesting**.

> Stem cell therapy could offer treatments for many people with chronic degenerative diseases. Stem cells could grow and replace damaged tissue in, e.g. the brains of Parkinson's sufferers. However, in order to research this area, scientists must create embryos which are then destroyed — they're only created so that their stem cells can be collected. This is, of course, highly controversial.

For: ....

....

Against: ....

....

Q3 Imagine a new drug has been developed to treat breast cancer. It has been tested on people with end-stage breast cancer, and shown to be an effective treatment with tolerable side effects.

a) The drug has not been tested on people with early-stage breast cancer.

    i) Why might someone with early-stage breast cancer want to take this drug?

    ....

    ii) Suggest why doctors would be unwilling to give this drug to patients with early-stage breast cancer.

    ....

b) An alternative treatment for breast cancer is radiotherapy. However, there are environmental issues, as well as unpleasant side effects, associated with radiotherapy. Outline one such issue.

....

Medical Research

Q4 Read the following extract from a newspaper article about a drug trial.

> Six men are tonight in a critical condition in hospital after taking part in a drug trial. The drug being tested was intended to treat chronic inflammatory conditions and leukaemia, but has instead left these men fighting for their lives. A spokesperson for the drug company involved has stressed that they followed all procedures correctly, including carrying out extensive laboratory studies before these trials began.

a) What might the **laboratory studies** have been?

....

b) Suggest why the laboratory studies did not predict the severe reaction seen in the patients.

....

....

c) Give one **positive outcome** of this test.

....

Q5 The cost in poorer countries of drugs for treating AIDS has recently fallen significantly. This is largely due to sales of **copies** of branded drugs, called **generic drugs**. These are cheaper because the company producing them did not have to pay the cost of the drug's development.

a) Explain how the sale of **generic drugs** might lead to the development of fewer new drugs.

....

....

b) Part a) gives an argument against making generic drugs. Outline one other argument **against** and one argument **for** the distribution of these drugs in poorer countries.

i) For: ....

....

ii) Against: ....

....

c) The drugs currently available treat the symptoms of AIDS, but do not cure the disease. Suggest one ethical issue that might arise if a cure for AIDS was being developed.

....

Mixed Questions — P3 Topic 6

Q1   One of Dr McLeod's patients has cancer and is being treated with **radiotherapy**.

a)   What sort of radiation would be used in this treatment?

....

b)   Describe how radiotherapy can help treat cancer.

....

c)   Dr McLeod thinks that the radiotherapy won't cure his patient's cancer,
but will reduce her suffering. What type of care is this? ....

d)   Dr McLeod hears about a new drug that might help his patient. The drug has not yet been tested
on cancer patients and the company is looking for volunteers to take part in a trial. Outline an
argument for and against this patient taking part in the trial.

For: ....

....

Against: ....

....

Q2   Mary has epilepsy. She is having a **PET scan** of her brain as part of a research study.
The researcher injects Mary with a radiotracer before scanning her brain.

a)   Describe what happens to the **positrons** emitted by the radiotracer in Mary's brain.

....

b)   Explain how **momentum** is **conserved** in this process.

....

....

....

Q3   Nurse Horton uses a **pulse oximeter** to monitor the blood
oxygen content of a patient who has recently had surgery.

a)   Describe and explain how a pulse oximeter works.

....

....

b)   If the blood has a high oxygen content, what colour will the oxyhaemoglobin appear?

....

Mixed Questions — P3 Topic 6

Q4   James's doctor thinks he may have a **cancerous tumour** in his intestine. James goes to hospital to have a PET scan of his abdomen.

a)   Before the PET scan, James is given an **injection**. What would this contain?

....

b)   The PET scan shows an area with much higher metabolic activity than the rest of the intestine. Could this area be **cancerous**? Explain your answer.

....

c)   The surgeon decides to investigate further using keyhole surgery.

   i)   Name the **instrument** the surgeon would use to see inside James's body. ....

   ii)   The instrument contains **optical fibres** to carry light into James's body and an image back out. Describe how light is carried along an optical fibre.

....

....

d)   During the operation James is connected to an **ECG** machine to monitor the activity of his heart.

   i)   What does an ECG measure?

....

   ii)   Sketch the shape of a typical ECG on the axes provided. Label the components of the curve.

[Graph with vertical axis "p.d. at electrodes" and horizontal axis "time (s)"]

e)   The time from peak to peak on James' ECG is **0.75 s**. What is his heart rate in beats per minute?

....

Q5   Karen has hurt her foot playing football. She is having an **X-ray** to find out whether she has broken a bone.

a)   The X-rays have an **intensity** of 430 W/m². The surface area of Karen's foot is 0.024 m². Calculate the approximate **power** of the radiation reaching Karen's foot.

....

b)   What does '**radiation**' mean?

....

c)   Karen is given special glasses to wear while the X-ray is taken. Explain why.

....

....

d)   The radiographer goes behind a lead screen while Karen has her X-ray. Why does he does this?

....

Mixed Questions — P3 Topic 6

Q6 An atom of nitrogen is bombarded with **proton radiation** in a cyclotron.

a) Why does this process need to take place in a cyclotron?

....

b) The nitrogen nucleus absorbs a proton. Why does this result in a new **element**?

....

c) The new element formed is an unstable isotope of carbon.
What sort of radiation would you expect it to emit?

....

Q7 Rob is using an EMG machine to measure the activity in the muscles of his arm when he lifts a
20 N weight. He lifts the weight onto a shelf, a vertical distance of 0.45 m then relaxes his arm.

a) Explain how an EMG machine measures muscle activity.

....

b) Calculate the **work** Rob does in lifting the weight once.

....

c) Rob now performs a set of 10 lifts in 24 s. Calculate the **power** he has generated.

....

....

d) Name one medical condition that EMG scans can help to diagnose. ....

Q8 A uranium-235 nucleus is bombarded with neutron radiation and absorbs a **thermal neutron**.

a) Write a nuclear equation to represent uranium-235 absorbing a thermal neutron.

....

b) The new uranium isotope is unstable and splits into two smaller atoms and two neutrons.
The uranium isotope was **stationary** before the fission took place.

i) What is the total **mass** of the fission products (in atomic mass units)?

....

ii) What is their total **momentum**? Give a reason for your answer.

....